The Little Guide to Giving Poster Presentations

The Little Guide to Giving Poster Presentations

Simple Steps to Success

John Bond

ROWMAN & LITTLEFIELD
Lanham • Boulder • New York • London

Published by Rowman & Littlefield
An imprint of The Rowman & Littlefield Publishing Group, Inc.
4501 Forbes Boulevard, Suite 200, Lanham, Maryland 20706
www.rowman.com

86-90 Paul Street, London EC2A 4NE, United Kingdom

British Library Cataloguing in Publication Information Available

Library of Congress Cataloging-in-Publication Data

Names: Bond, John, 1960– author.
Title: The little guide to giving poster presentations : simple steps to success /
  John Bond.
Description: Lanham : Rowman & Littlefield, [2023] | Includes bibliographical
  references and index. | Summary: "The Little Guide to Giving a Poster
  Presentation: Simple Steps to Success is a practical step-by-step guide for the
  novice or uncertain author on giving a poster presentation"— Provided by
  publisher.
Identifiers: LCCN 2023019722 (print) | LCCN 2023019723 (ebook) | ISBN
  9781475870152 (paperback) | ISBN 9781475870169 (epub)
Subjects: LCSH: Poster presentations. | Posters. | Visual communication. |
  Communication in learning and scholarship. | Teaching—Aids and devices. |
  Academic writing.
Classification: LCC NC1815 .B66 2023 (print) | LCC NC1815 (ebook) | DDC
  744.3—dc23/eng/20230602
LC record available at https://lccn.loc.gov/2023019722
LC ebook record available at https://lccn.loc.gov/2023019723

This book is dedicated to the future poster presenter, author, and researcher: Nora Bond.

Contents

Foreword

A 3-Credit Course in a Book

A poster presentation. Sounds so simple and perhaps even elementary to some in the academic community. Yet to others, the creation of a poster, let alone the actual presentation of the content, can be a daunting task. Most of us professors have seen hundreds if not thousands of posters in passing during our conference travels, but rarely do we spend quality time honing the skills necessary to showcase that poster that stands out to everyone as simply impressive. Impressive in its appearance, impressive in the content, and impressive in the delivery.

I have known John Bond for some twenty-five years. During this time, we have already had a very successful professional relationship, in my role as an author and John's role as publisher. However, like any other trusting business relationship, a mutual respect and established friendship makes for greater outcomes. The first day I met John, I realized how little I knew about professional writing. Literally every time we met or spoke to each other, I would always pick up another pointer. Yet the pointer came later in the conversation following John's inquiry of my family, my travels, my health, and anything else nonprofessionally related. Why is this important for you as a reader of this book to know? Because I trust John Bond. I have come to learn that whatever John says, or in this case writes, is conveyed not only with experience and guidance but also with sincerity and compassion for one to trust and heed such advice.

When I first learned he wrote a book on giving a poster presentation, I must admit I wondered "how does John know about this topic?" After all, we had never discussed poster presentations. When I was asked by John to provide a review for the book, I was highly anxious to see what was included. And truth be told it wasn't so that I could critique the work and reveal that this wasn't John's space. In fact, quite the opposite. I knew that anything John touched and developed would be nothing less than an absolutely marvelous book. And as I expected, after myself preparing and presenting hundreds of posters in various formats all over the world, I was not disappointed. I wish I had this resource twenty-five years ago!

One gains a fascinating appreciation from John's work in this book that makes me wonder should this in fact be an entire 3-credit course. Defining the topic clearly, having the ideal content layout and visual appearance, identifying the most appropriate and beneficial place to submit and present, to knowing how to transition your poster into a peer-reviewed publication in an impactful journal. Wow, most of us only learn this in school by observing our mentors and gaining the necessary skills as we go. Like all else in life, such an approach has its advantages, but nothing can top the formal and its foundation of best practices.

The Little Guide to Giving Poster Presentations is a resource that should be on every student's desk, regardless of whether one is an undergraduate preparing the first-ever poster or a postdoctoral student with previous experience. In fact, all faculty should take the time to read this as there is something between the covers that I truly believe can be a valuable addition to one's existing knowledge. It was a pleasure to learn from John Bond once again. Trust me, this is a book you do not want to pass over!

Jeff G. Konin, PhD, ATC, PT, FACSM, FNATA
Clinical Professor, Florida International University
Director, Doctor of Athletic Training Program, FIU
President, Konin Consulting, LLC
Founder and Partner, The Rehberg Konin Group

Preface

Helping Authors Communicate Their Message

There are many opportunities open to researchers, academics, postdocs, and students to disseminate their research and work to the wider world. I have worked with key figures in their field as well as students just getting started. Many have been based in North America and Europe but also in Pakistan, Uruguay, and the Philippines. They all share one thing in common: the desire to be part of the intellectual discourse in their community.

But there are barriers to participating in an activity like giving a poster presentation: free time, limited resources, being new to a field, and the requisite knowledge. This book addresses the last one: how to give poster presentations. The book guides those with a desire to present their work in simple steps.

I have worked for over thirty years in scholarly publishing: as an editor, publisher, chief content officer, author, mentor, and writing and publishing consultant. See the "About the Author" section at the end of the book to learn more about my background including my YouTube channel (which has over one hundred videos on scholarly publishing topics you might find of interest). I have overseen the publishing of 20,000 journal articles and 500 books in my career and written six books myself. I have attended over 100 poster presentations across a wide range of disciplines and spoken with countless presenters. My most recent book is a companion to this one: *The Little Guide to Getting Your Journal Article Published: Simple Steps to Success.*

But by far my greatest accomplishment is the privilege of having worked with an array of interesting authors on spreading their message and research.

I decided to write this book as a response to so many clients who had many questions about the process of giving a poster presentation. This slim volume lays out the step-by-step process to taking the big step of presenting your work as a poster. With attention to detail and hard work, I know you will be successful. Good luck and let me know when you have presented your poster!

John Bond

Acknowledgments

This book is an accumulation of knowledge that I have gained over the last thirty-plus years. I have learned so much from so many people. From the first professional conference I attended in Baltimore, to the first poster presentation I browsed while looking for book authors, to speaking with authors one-on-one, I have been the beneficiary of so much practical knowledge and hard-fought wisdom. I am at a loss at how to acknowledge so many people who taught me so much.

One group I can acknowledge is the very generous reviewers of the manuscript for this book: Lori T. Andersen, EdD, OTR/L, FAOTA; Emily Compagnoni, RN, BSN; Nancy Doyle, OTD, OTR/L; Ben Finio, PhD; Liat Gafni-Lachter, PhD, OTD, OTR/L; Jeff Konin, PhD, ATC, PT, FACSM, FNATA; David Klassen, PhD, and others. They all provided valuable, detailed suggestions. Any shortcomings in the book, however, are mine and do not reflect on them.

My thanks as well to support and encouragement from Bill Carrigan, PhD; Luke Holbrook, PhD; Mary Law, PhD, OT(C), FCAOT, FCAHS, OC; Beth Linkewich, CHE, MPA, OT Reg (Ontario); Cori McMahon, PsyD, NCCE; Eric Schmieder, ME; Lori Smith Okon, MS; Gerald Arnell Williams, MS; and Michele Yelman, RN.

I gained the most from my valued, former colleagues at SLACK Incorporated. Thank you for what I learned, and sometimes had to relearn.

Finally, thank you as always to the ever-supportive Theresa Woolley. None of this is possible without you.

Introduction

How to Use This Book

Poster presentations are foundational to scholarly communication. Many times, it is the first step for new or aspiring academics in sharing their work with the wider world. These presentations are the grandparent (or child) of many great journal articles, grants, monographs, or research careers.

The goal of this book is to learn how to take your ideas and research and offer them in the form of a poster presentation, whether in person or virtual. The book proceeds in a step-by-step fashion. Read the entire book once. Then go back and review the key parts, making your personalized plan for the necessary steps as you proceed.

This book is (mostly) discipline- or subject-matter neutral. It is not a book just for STEM, the social sciences, or a specific subject area. Many of the concepts are universal. In some places, additional work on your part is needed to adapt these concepts to your particular subject matter.

This book is about academic poster presentations. There are other forms of scholarly communication such as journal articles, monographs, and more that all have value in the ecosphere of knowledge. These other formats are not addressed here.

In regard to language in the book, I use the terms author, presenter, and researcher interchangeably as they represent the various hats you will wear through the process. Also, I use the terms audience, conference attendee, and reader to mean the same person with whom you will interact. I have chosen to write this book in the familiar fashion ("when you are writing . . .") instead of the more academic form ("when one is writing . . ."). The book is meant to be a conversation between us. I hope you enjoy it.

John Bond

Part I

GETTING STARTED

Chapter 1

What Is a Poster Presentation?

Nothing in life is to be feared, it is only to be understood.
—Marie Curie

A poster presentation is one of the fundamental forms of academic or scholarly communication. An author or researcher presents their findings or materials in a defined or limited manner. Typically, the author creates a poster of a standard size (e.g., 4 feet by 6 feet or 1 meter by 2 meters) and presents their findings in a standard format (e.g., three columns with distinct parts for each section of content such as research or conclusions). The poster is usually presented at a conference where many attendees might view and digest the materials being presented by the author.

Poster presentations are focused on specific findings or ideas. They are not journal articles shrunk down with no changes. They are rarely as broad as a peer-reviewed journal article or oral presentation at a conference. Posters can present research data, general information, or take a position on important topics being discussed in a field of research.

Posters are often very visual and may contain important figures or images that get to the heart of their material. Concentrating on images is helpful as many of the attendees at a conference may have limited time to absorb complex material. Truly, a picture (image or table) is worth a thousand words when it comes to a poster presentation.

Getting the balance (text and images) "just right" is key. A conference full of all text posters is nearly as bad as posters that are all images without key data that ties it all together. Balance is vital.

Poster presentations are, "One part billboard, one part research paper" ("Effective Poster Presentations," 2022).

Posters have been physical posters for decades but recently they have also been presented in digital form, sometimes called ePosters. This allows a far greater number of people to interact with the materials. Also, more engaging formats such as video or animations can be included in this option. At some conferences, posters may be presented in both physical paper and digital format. Undoubtedly, more poster presentations will be migrating to the digital format in the future because of the increased availability to many more individuals. This will also be occurring because these presentations can then be archived and live on much, much longer than a paper poster that is made available for only a few hours at a conference.

The content of a poster presentation may be just a small section of the larger work being done by the author. It may focus on one interesting or unique aspect that can be captured in this short communication format. Poster presentations may lead to the eventual publication of a journal article or an oral presentation at a future conference or meeting. These additional scholarly communication/publishing opportunities might include part, or all of the work displayed on the poster presentation.

Poster presentations many times take place at professional or educational conferences or venues. They may be local, regional, national, or international. These conferences may be presented by a professional society/association or an institution. Sometimes they take place at an annual meeting, other times they may be topic- or theme-based. These conferences may include oral sessions and other educational presentations in addition to the area devoted to posters. Sometimes there are poster presentations on a much smaller scale, for instance, taking place within an institution and therefore less formatted and less intimidating. These smaller-scale ones are great opportunities for students or those new to the format.

To present a poster at a conference, an author would typically need to submit their work or ideas to a committee designated by the organizers of the event. This submission may be an abstract of the work with some other key details. The committee would then peer review the work and decide which posters to include in the event. An author would need to attend the conference and, likely, need funding for these activities. Authors may seek out funds from their institution, apply for or use grant money they have previously secured, or pay for the activity themselves.

Poster presentations are widely used in the STEM fields (science, technology, engineering, and mathematics) as well as some major areas of the humanities (e.g., history, education, and languages).

Poster presentations are an essential part of scholarly communications. Now, why should you consider giving one?

Chapter 2

Why Give a Poster Presentation?

Whether you think you can or think you can't, you're right.
—Henry Ford

Academics and researchers lead complex and busy lives. There are innumerable ways for them to spend their "free time." Is giving a poster presentation a valuable use of the precious commodity of time? Most times the answer to broad questions like this would be "it depends." However, in this instance, the answer is nearly an unqualified "yes."

Poster presentations help you:

- Disseminate your work and ideas.
- Get involved in the conversation taking place in your field.
- Get valuable feedback from other like-minded people or experts about your work, potentially allowing it to expand. Conversely, feedback can allow you to see flaws in rationale, methodology, and more.
- Learn about the publishing process.
- Start on the road to new publishing adventures such as writing a journal article, writing a book chapter, writing or editing a monograph or book, giving presentations at conferences, applying for a grant, and more.
- Experience and navigate peer review and related submission systems.
- Meet like-minded professionals interested in your subject area, thereby expanding your network. These people may be future collaborators or coauthors.

- Add a meaningful activity to your curriculum vitae.
- (Potentially) Contribute toward promotion or tenure requirements (check with your institution).
- Apply for or expand future grant funding.
- Sharpen your public speaking as well as dialectic skills.
- And many other intangibles.

By giving a poster presentation, you are in esteemed company. Almost all veteran authors, researchers, and academics have given poster presentations. For most of them, this may have been their first step in their publishing/communications journey. Likely many continue giving poster presentations throughout their careers. In 2022, there was a great Tweet with a photo of Nobel Prize–winner John O'Keefe giving a poster presentation at the Society for Neuroscience.

Of course, poster preparation and presentation take time and likely funding (more about this later). But all good things come at a cost. On the whole though, the effort to apply for and give a poster presentation is well worth it from an academic and career advancement point of view. Now, let us get started.

Chapter 3

Defining Your Topic

Everything has been thought of before, but the problem is to think of it again. —*Johann Wolfgang von Goethe*

You have been doing research or work on a new idea, perhaps alone or with a collaborator. Maybe colleagues and or supervisors have encouraged you to start to share it. And then information just arrived in your mailbox/inbox about an upcoming conference which has poster presentation opportunities. Maybe you saw a call for submissions. You are going to take the plunge and submit an abstract!

Let us start at the beginning and assume you are immersed in a project, research, or some scholarly endeavor that you want to share. Your first step will be to define the idea or topic for your poster.

First, is your work new or unique? This question will be one of the criteria that reviewers will use when considering your poster. No conference wants to offer work that goes over the same ground as other work in the field.

Second, focus on one single message or concept. Do not attempt a complex or multifaceted approach. It may seem trite but be able to summarize your findings into a short elevator ride. Ideally, be able to explain your idea in one or two sentences. No poster can encompass all your work, all your research, or an entire complex study. If you try to include it all, you will lose your audience.

Third, quality is the key to getting your poster accepted. It is tempting early in your career to simply want to get accepted. Do not be short-sighted. The goal should be to make a difference.

Using these three criteria, you will move on to developing a thesis statement. A thesis statement presents your main idea or central message. The argument you intend to make should be reflected in this statement. It can usually be expressed in a single sentence. The thesis statement helps to organize and develop the entire poster.

Once you have developed this statement, refer to it each time you return to the tasks at hand for writing and poster creation. Let it guide you in everything you do. Post it at your workspace.

Remember, your entire poster needs to support the thesis statement. When deciding what to include and not include, use the thesis statement as the benchmark. Do not let your poster become a litany of somewhat-related facts on your topic; it should be a supporting document to your thesis statement.

When developing your poster, in many fields, reproducibility is critical. There has been significant discussion in academia over reproducibility these last few years. Consider how your work will stand up to the scrutiny of others.

Also, consider metadata, which is the descriptive information about a published item. It is used for discovery and identification purposes. It includes elements such as title, author, and (most importantly) keywords or terms. Think about how your work or poster can and will be classified. Some of these terms are self-evident yet not always included in a poster application, title, or abstract. Metadata or keywords drive the scholarly communication and publishing world.

Finally, when deciding on all of these essential points, ask yourself two questions. What one takeaway do you want the audience to leave with and why should anyone be interested in your poster? These hard questions should guide your choices.

Chapter 4

Writing Your Title and Abstract

If any man wish to write in a clear style, let him be first clear in his thoughts. —Johann Wolfgang von Goethe

You have defined your topic and have a thesis statement. Now let us grow that into the next important elements.

Most conference organizers will require you to submit a summary or abstract of your proposed poster. This is your next step. All abstracts usually come with a word limit or range. Some use 250 words, others a few more or a few less (Andrade, 2011). All word-processing software readily gives word counts for any document or section of a document.

Abstracts are tricky because of the word limits. They take your complex, multidimensional work and condense it into very, very few words. You are not explaining your entire work or findings. It is just the highlights.

It should cover:

- What your poster is all about.
- Why your findings/research are important.
- What work or research you did to arrive at your conclusions.
- Why your work is novel or unique.
- The conclusion or the big takeaway from the poster.

If possible (and there may not be room), add in how your work fits into the current thinking on your topic.

In *most* cases, there will not be room to cite other works.

A reminder about the discussion in the previous chapter about keywords or terms—make sure important subject matter terms are included as space allows. These also help position your work within the discipline and help tremendously with any searches your audience might make.

Spend way too much time on abstract creation and editing. Show it to colleagues, mentors, and others and have them give you feedback on it. Be open to all ideas. There may be time later to revise or change the abstract, but you will want it to be (for now) as good as you can make it. This abstract or summary might be the sole item the poster presentation committee uses to decide whether to include your work. Pressure! But if you have confidence in your work, then let the chips fall where they may.

Another important step at this point is coming up with the title for the poster. This may seem deceptively simple, but do not be fooled. The title, even more so than the abstract, can be used to judge your work. As your audience streams by your poster someday, they will glance at the title, and it will have to draw them in.

Of course, you want the title to be accurate and professional. These are givens. But you are also looking to have a compelling and interesting title. Try to get to the heart of what your work is about, knowing it cannot replace the abstract or even the poster. Some professions lean more toward label titles while others may skew toward questions. In some fields, they might even be provocative. Scan other poster presentations in your field to get a sense of the norm. As with the abstract, spend way too much time thinking about this.

Have your title be ten words or less. Sometimes this may be a challenge but be concise. If it is too long, your audience may either skip it or get confused.

Consider making a list of possible titles, knowing they will be using many of the same terms. Be creative and open. Then when you have a list of maybe a dozen possible titles, start to rank them by what works best. Show them to friends or colleagues to get their opinions. Ask them to vote on their choice. This will also give you insight into how your poster may be interpreted (or misinterpreted).

Titles are very subjective, but it is easy to see when some of them go awry. Here is a list of (fictional) poster presentation titles and some commentary about what is right or wrong. When you read them, form your opinion as to what you like and do not like about each one:

- A Novel Approach to Exercise (*too generic, not enough details*)
- Hospice Care Education (*same, narrow down your focus*)
- Rice Production in Thailand (*better but can still add specifics here*)
- The Relationship Between Academia and Practice (*while you will know what subject area because you are at a conference, if this poster comes up in an online search, it is too broad for anyone to be interested in pursuing it*)
- Poster by John Bond (*we know, but this is the place to tell us what your poster is about*)
- Developing a Novel Gene-Sequencing Technique (*better*)
- Modeling and Analysis of Educational Processes in Math (*better*)
- The Effect of Outreach on HMO Enrollment with an Underserved Population (*nicely done*)
- Economic Development Zones in Alabama (*specific but probably room to add a couple more words*)
- The Effects of Conflicting Auditory Clues on Comprehension in Students with ADHD (*very nice*)
- Identifying Biomarkers to Improve Personalized Treatment of MS (*very nice*)
- Antibiotic Scaffolding (*this is more a label than title*)
- Identifying Marine Microbes in Waste Runoff (*nice*)
- Temperature and Mating Patterns in *T. migratorius* (*very specific*)
- Physiological Responses to Sudden Withdrawal of Antianxiety Medication (*very descriptive*)

A key concept for both the abstract and title are to hold nothing back. Some novice authors or researchers want to hold back the big conclusion for those who experience the full text. This is a mistake. Many people will only ever encounter the title and abstract, perhaps in an online database. They need to know what conclusions you came to and not have them held back like a surprise ending in a movie.

You have a title and abstract, now let us discuss who your audience is.

Chapter 5

Who Is Your Target Audience?

If you would be a reader, read; if a writer, write. —Epictetus

It is essential to know who the audience will be for your poster presentation. This will help you tailor your idea, title, and abstract to ensure it hits the mark with them.

Look closely at the society or institution that will be presenting the conference. Sometimes there will be an "About" section at their website that breaks down the demographics of its members. Some large conferences also have a demographic breakdown for attendees. This data will be a goldmine for understanding who you will be interacting with. Of course, not everyone who attends the conference will walk by your poster, or even attend the presentations, but this is a start. Also, conferences sometimes may be topic based. This information will help you to focus and determine if this event is the right place for you and your work. If your work is not a good match for the group or meeting, consider looking elsewhere.

Look at the backgrounds of the people who have previously presented posters. This will help give you an insight into what the conference organizers are looking for.

Most conferences will at least add poster abstracts to their websites. Abstracts also may end up being indexed in important databases. This would be a great side benefit. If this might be the case, your audience greatly expands.

When considering an audience, do not just think about the person's profession but also the stage of their career. Even within a profession or subject area, your material may be of greater interest to people in the early stage of their career or to people with more experience.

Choosing an exact group when creating your presentation will increase the engagement with your material.

Do not try to tailor your presentation toward everyone. This will only ensure it being of interest to no one. Targeting an ideal audience will be beneficial to you during the writing process by keeping your message focused.

By choosing an ideal reader, you are not discounting secondary audiences. These other groups may be interested in your topic, and they may seek out and value your presentation. Even if they are not the primary audience, they will still likely have the technical knowledge and interest for them to appreciate your material. They are still secondary, and you cannot completely consider them for all key decisions.

With this and all future scholarly communication efforts, knowing who your audience or reader is will continue to be valuable. Always keep this point at the top of your list when starting on a new project. Now, let us move on to finding a place to present your work.

Part II

SECURING POSTER PRESENTATION OPPORTUNITIES

Chapter 6

Finding Venues to Present

If your actions inspire others to dream more, learn more, do more and become more, you are a leader. —John Quincy Adams

Let us take a step back. You have summarized your idea and developed a thesis statement for it. You have written an abstract and a title for your poster presentation and shown it to friends and colleagues for feedback. You have identified your target audience. Now is the time to find a place to present the poster.

You likely have an opportunity in mind already but, in case you do not, let us look at some:

- Large conferences or conventions: Whether national or international, the meetings of the professional societies in your field are great opportunities. These are usually prestige occasions. They many times offer poster presentations on multiple days with multiple sessions. The number of posters actually offered may be several thousand. They are likely very well organized and also competitive. Go to your society's annual meeting's home page and look for information about the educational or academic opportunities they offer. Your first efforts may not be on this scale, but do not discount this as a possibility. Your ideas and work will be the final determinant, not your stature in the association. Having said this, always consider being a member of the primary organization in your field. It offers great educational and networking opportunities.

- Regional conferences: Many aspiring presenters start with state or regional conferences. These may be more manageable from a cost and travel perspective. The quality of the work offered many times can rival national conferences. These may also be less competitive for the person seeking their first opportunity.
- Institutional symposiums or meetings: Local universities, health-care centers, governmental bodies, and other organizations may organize conferences, many times topic-based. These may be the best chances to do a poster presentation. They also give great networking opportunities to find like-minded people in your field. They also may raise your profile from a career perspective.
- Departmental meetings: Some very large institutions may have large subsections of departments. These may also be a great opportunity to give a poster.

By keeping an eye open on these venues, you will likely find many places to consider presenting your poster. But there are other ways to find out about places to present.

- Networking: By talking to others in your institution, department, or circle of colleagues, you will expand your chance of hearing about conferences. Tell them you are interested in presenting your recent work and ask them to keep an eye out for you.
- Tell your supervisor: Many times, this person is tuned in to many different areas. They may be your best eyes and ears, as well as know of interdisciplinary opportunities that suit your work.
- Watch for "Call for posters" or "Call for papers": These communications may be issued by the organizations listed above. They will give details including topic focus, deadline, and presentation specifics/locations. Try doing an internet search for calls in your field. A side note about something called predatory publishing—in recent years, some organizations have popped up that offer to publish your work for a fee, but they provide no service and no real value. When you do find an opportunity through a search, make sure it is from a recognized or well-respected organization.

Remember that these opportunities might be in person or virtual. Both are equally valuable and offer many of the same benefits. Read more about virtual versus in-person later in this book.

By focusing on the best fit for your work or topic with the conference or theme of the event, you will increase the likelihood of acceptance. Do not choose one because you will probably be able to present but apply for those that matter and that will showcase your work.

Some fortunate few may not need to look for presentation opportunities or applicable conferences and tend to all the details involved with submission. An experienced person they work with may come in one day and say, "Here is a good opportunity for you to present your work. Why don't you apply for it?" If you are in this situation, appreciate the person handing you the opportunity but know it may not always be like this.

A point to consider is where you are in *your* career, and where that puts you in relation to the audience. Your approach will be different if you are a young graduate student getting your feet wet and looking for speaking experience, compared to a senior graduate student or postdoc who is on the job market and looking for some serious networking.

So you have narrowed down a couple of venues to submit your work to. How are you going to pay for it?

Chapter 7

Finding Funding for Your Presentation

A benefactor is a representative of God. —Benjamin Whichcote

There is no doubt that giving poster presentations can advance your research and career. It offers networking and professional opportunities, but it does come at a cost.

First, let us look at what these costs are and then how you might get funding for them. Perhaps the top expense might be the registration fee to attend the conference. For national or international conferences, this fee can be significant. This fee may be lessened if you are a member of the organizing body (which is itself an expense). Some groups might lessen the registration fee for individuals who are presenting. Sometimes this includes poster presenters, other times it does not. If your poster is accepted and the group does not volunteer a reduced registration fee, ask them anyway.

After the registration fee, travel is likely the next biggest expense. Flights, hotels, meals, transportation at the location, and others costs quickly add up. If the location is a destination location like New York, San Francisco, London, or Tokyo (good news and bad news) then the costs can be significantly higher. But look at the experience you will have!

The other hidden expense is your time. Being at a conference can eat up a big chunk of your work week. This time out of your office might be professional but sometimes it might be vacation or comp time. And there is all that work and research not getting done.

Sample costs can vary widely. Here is a brief look at what they may run:

- Conference registration: ranges from free (some waive the fee for presenters) to $1,500 or more. Perhaps $250 to $500 is an average for presenters.
- Travel: this may be as little as gas or a subway ticket up to an airline ticket. Local: perhaps $100 for parking or travel. Airfare: domestic, perhaps $250 to $1,000. The likely average is $500. International, $1,500 and up.
- Hotel: accommodations vary in quality as well, including distance from the event. Perhaps from $150 to $500 per night. Consider $250 an average which includes taxes and other fees.
- Meals: perhaps $50 a day, and up.
- Incidentals: perhaps figure $25 a day for unexpected expenses.
- Your time out of the office and the value your presentation presents for your career? Priceless.

When you have a handle on these costs, develop a budget. This may be only for your information so you know what you are getting yourself into or it may be to request funding.

Depending on your circumstances, you might be able to ask for funding from your institution. It may be partial, or they may have an educational fund for just these opportunities.

If your work is grant-funded, the grant might cover presentations like this. Check with the funding body to see if there are additional funds available outside the grant.

All of these groups have a vested interest in your presenting and your work being disseminated. Whether it is your institution or a grant funder, when you present about your work, their goals are advanced. Your efforts are the best public relations for these groups. Include this point in any funding request.

Sometimes the conference may either reduce registration fees or have small first-time presenter grants. Ask the organizers.

Universities sometimes have small grants for junior faculty or for initiatives such as international presentations. Additionally, you should justify the benefit to your employer/institution when presenting the budget so it goes beyond your benefit.

Part of developing a budget and seeking funding is to determine whether a poster presentation is worth your time. In essence, is it a good return on your (time) investment? However, part of the calculation is not quantifiable. Getting started on your wider academic and research career and gaining valuable skills when interacting with other like-minded people in your field cannot have a number attached to it. Keep this in mind when you make your decision.

In some fields, there is no worry about funding because of industries that have a vested interest in the work. Others struggle through with little industry, institutional, or grant funding. This is a challenge, but nonetheless the need for presenting your work persists.

Chapter 8

Creating and Submitting Your Poster Presentation Proposal

Details make perfection, and perfection is not a detail.
—Leonardo da Vinci

You have a target event that you would like to present at, including a budget. Now it is time to submit an application. The website with the conference details or the call for posters will likely have all of the information on submitting your application.

The submission process for posters is usually less structured than it is for peer-review journal articles. The processes can range widely. The organizers may require you to submit an application form, or they may just provide an email address where you can send your relevant material. You might also need to register with the website. The information that is required might include:

- Name and contact details of all the people involved in the poster. You may need to designate one person as the corresponding author.
- Professional qualifications, including academic background.
- Current area of research or academic interests.
- An abstract or description of your poster. The 250-word abstract that you previously created will serve you well now. Organizers may ask for as little as twenty-five or fifty words so you may need to edit your full abstract down to the required amount. Sometimes the abstract target amount is based on characters versus words. See the next chapter for the importance of this abstract or description.

- References, gap analysis, methods, findings, and more.
- More information on your project, such as grant funding.

You may need to agree to some of their terms. First would be to attend the conference, including the times for presentation. Another might be to verify that you are eligible, which might mean you are a member of the society (not always required), have a certain level of academic accomplishment, or have a certain level of certification (such as being a registered physician). Many times, your abstract or the poster might appear at the organizer's website or in a program book associated with the meeting. Sometimes your abstract will also be included in abstracting and indexing services or databases such as Google Scholar, PubMed/MEDLINE, EBSCO, ProQuest, and others. This helps spread the word about your work and would be initiated by the conference organizer. You will be granting permission to include your materials. Finally, you may need to sign a conflict of interest or disclosure statement.

Authorship is an important concept in publishing and scholarly communication. The people associated with your poster should be the creators and the people that did the work—no more or less. Unfortunately, the practice in the past has been to add some people in a department, even if they did no work. Also, some junior people might be left off a poster, even though they contributed. Because of this, organizers may ask you to affirm that the people listed are the ones (and only the ones) who created the work.

As previously discussed, some conferences are topic-focused. Some days or sessions of the poster presentations may also have a topic or subtopic focus. If this is true, make sure your submission dovetails with the topic. Try to connect them, but do not overreach.

Double-check all of the materials you are submitting for completeness. Make sure you run a spelling and grammar check. Quality counts when the organizers are deciding who to include in their conference.

Be mindful of all deadlines. After all this work, you do not want to miss the application date or any of the other dates associated with the process.

Submissions for consideration will be reviewed by a jury or committee that will consider your poster presentation. This is usually done in a blind fashion. Try not to use institutional or identifying names in your abstract for this reason. This committee will choose the best or most appropriate presentations for their conference. The time from application to when the committee decides may be a few weeks or months. Be patient. The corresponding author will hear about the verdict. If it is a go, start working on your poster and presentation. If they do not accept it, no worries. Every great author has been rejected in the past. Try again or reenvision your work.

Chapter 9

Giving Your Idea the Best Pitch

Wherever you go, go with all your heart. —Confucius

"Pitch" connotes to many the sales process. All material needs to draw the reader in, and your application to present, the poster itself, and all future writing are no exceptions.

Many authors and readers of academic material accept that the writing style can be dry. The content and facts may be fascinating or engaging, but not the presentation. This does not have to be the case. Of course, your writing will not be flowery, but there is a middle ground between dry (and dull) and short story writing.

In your application or description of your poster presentation, you have an opportunity to separate yourself from the pack. This is true for longer abstracts and the rest of the text on your poster. Become an astute reader of academic work and you will start to see the difference.

You are telling a story (albeit a detailed one) about the work you are involved with. Take your time to engage the reader; draw them in. Take the reader or audience from start to finish by seeing the text as a whole. Your work should not be "list fact 1," then "list fact 2," then . . .

This is a fine line. There are word and format restrictions. You have a set of facts that need to be related to the reader, but do not settle for choppy, bulleted sentences that seem computer-generated.

Anything you write should be read aloud. It is a powerful practice to ensure accuracy but also flow. Another tip is to have a (smart) friend read your work—someone who is not an expert in your field. They

31

should follow the essence of what you are trying to convey. Ask them to relate back to your point and also to note any places where the writing was dense or tortured.

Accuracy and honesty are key. But please consider that your writing can engage people (or not), and this may influence your poster's acceptance and whether the audience engages with it or not.

Most importantly, follow the abstract proposal guidelines exactly. This is not always a given, as they vary significantly.

As you progress in your academic and writing career, clarity of thought becomes even more essential. Some good books on writing and editing are listed in the bibliography at the end of this book.

Part III

CREATING YOUR MESSAGE

Chapter 10

Developing a Plan and Timeline

A journey of a thousand miles begins with a single step. —*Lao Tzu*

You have been accepted to present a poster at an upcoming conference. Congratulations. Now you have to finish what you started and turn your extended abstract into a poster. Simple? It can be.

Starting with a plan and timeline will make the process much smoother and produce better results. A sample Poster Presentation Planning Guide is provided at the end of this book.

Create detailed steps addressing each task to be done. Make each step granular. Working in small chunks can help make the process manageable. Consider using a spreadsheet to track these tasks and your plan. Spreadsheets allow you to add or edit as your work progresses. Start to develop your task list now and add to it as you proceed through this book. The list should be updated throughout the whole process. It can also be helpful to keep a running to-do list.

Next is adding a realistic timeline. For each step in the plan, assign dates for completion. You might consider assigning an exact time of day and the length of time you allot to it.

The timeline needs to be realistic. Being overly optimistic or pessimistic does not serve you well. You should have a firm end date for submission and then presentation. The end date will likely be the organizer's submission deadline. Keep yourself accountable to the schedule you create. Of course, bumps in the road will occur, and you may miss a date, but a commitment is a commitment. You must chisel away at the project if you are going to complete the poster before it is to be presented. Creating regular work habits is a key to your ongoing writing and publishing success. Set times and stick to them.

When creating a schedule, incremental steps are more valuable than big blocks of time, which are likely to be borrowed from when other tasks in your life demand your attention. Do not just block out time on your calendar to "write." There are other theories that finding large blocks of quiet time is best. This is like exercising at the gym and a schedule will serve you the best in the long run.

There are some great apps that can help you keep track of your tasks and schedule. They will graphically show your progress and remind you of your commitment to the project. You likely have apps like this available through your smartphone, desk, or laptop. Alternatively, search productivity apps for the best ones. Consider using one of these powerful tools.

All conferences have deadlines, and they must be followed. Working backward can help you realize the time you have available.

Developing a plan and the accompanying timeline is one of the most concrete steps you can take to keep you on track for creating your poster. Only by seeing that the process is composed of individual tasks can you conquer any concerns you have about your ability to achieve your goal. Studiously work the plan! You will be pleased you did.

Chapter 11

Understanding the Parts of a Poster

The whole is greater than the sum of its parts. —Anonymous

Likely, you have had experience with viewing posters in the past. So, it is straightforward turning your work into a poster, right? Not so fast. Let us review the parts to ensure that we are moving toward the same goal.

The organizers will provide the specifications for your poster. If you get nothing else from this chapter, find these guidelines for your presentation and *follow them exactly.*

Start with understanding whether your poster will be a physical or digital presentation, or both. If the answer is both, will they be separate designs and layouts (likely) or identical file formats?

A poster can have a vertical or horizontal orientation (portrait or landscape). Understand how it will be mounted: on a table, on a wall, or standing on the floor.

The poster will have to be an exact dimension. A common size would be 4 feet by 6 feet (or 1 meter by 2 meters). Make sure you find out the size from the start. Also, ensure which of the dimensions is width and which is height.

The poster will be laid out in two, three, or four columns. Next will be the direction of the content in the columns. Will the audience read all the way through column one and then move on to column two? Or will the audience read from left to right and then go down to the second row (figure 11.1)? More to come on this important difference.

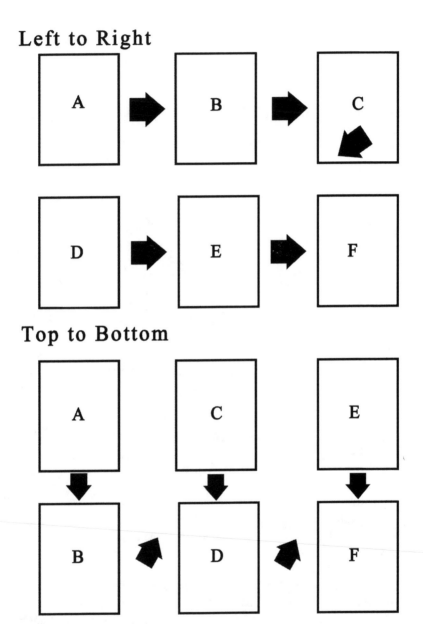

Figure 11.1.   Order of Content

Your poster will consist of text and images. The text should be structured so the audience knows what to expect. The guidelines will likely give exact details on this structured format but let us look at the most common textual elements:

- The title: A crucial part. It can include a title and subtitle (the subtitle is the part after the colon). As discussed, consider the audience's quick read of the title and their decision to review the rest of the material. Use keywords that will attract the attention of the in-person reader as well as those searching online. Some titles can get really long, so be concise. It does not need to include the sum total of your work.
- The authors: This is usually right below the title. Include only those individuals that did work on the project. Make sure everyone agrees on the order. Include all degrees to let the reader know your background. Include affiliations as required or as space allows. This can be disciplinary specific, so check in your field to see what is expected. Sometimes the logo or the institution's name will be included as well. More on this later.
- Abstract: The abstract is a brief summary or synopsis of your work as presented in the poster. It is used to help the audience determine their interest in what you accomplished. It may seem like a given to include your abstract on the poster but pause for a moment. Abstracts in long journal articles make sense. Readers use them to judge if they should spend the time reading it. But your poster is so short, is including an abstract wise? Some experts say "yes" to including one, and some say "no." Also, some organizers may mandate its use (or absence). Look at other posters in your field and see what the common practice is. When in doubt, leave it out. Readers will understand your work quickly after absorbing the introduction and more.
- Organizational structure or document format headings: This is a generic term for how you might structure your presentation. This expected format may vary by discipline or subject area. One common document format is IMRaD ("IMRAD," 2022). Check with your colleagues or the published literature in your field to see if they use this one or others. No matter the discipline, most academic work follows the IMRaD format in concept but may use different terms or labels

Table 11.1. Sample Organizational Headings in Six Subject Areas

Zoology	Zoology	Education	Education
Introduction	Abstract	Background	Abstract
Hypothesis	Introduction	Methodology	Background
Prediction	Habitat Factors	Population Sample	Methodology
Results	Population	Key Findings	Results
Methods	Response	Goals	Conclusions
Discussion	Conclusions	Successes	
The Future		Challenges	
		Recommendations	

Medicine	Medicine	Health	Health
Introduction	Background	Introduction	Motivation
Study Design	Hypothesis	Methods	Methods
Baseline	Measures	Results	Evaluating Data
Follow Up	Results	Conclusions	Tools
Predictions	Conclusions		
Outcomes			

Economics	Economics	Biotechnology	Biotechnology
Overview	Abstract	Abstract	Introduction
Objective	Introduction	Introduction	Materials and Methods
Data	Research Questions	Methods	Results
Model	Methods	Pathways	Conclusions
Results	Results	Results	Enhancements
Policy Implications	Conclusions	Discussion	
		Future Direction	

Note the variance of approach even within a subject.

for each section; IMRaD stands for introduction, methods, results, and discussion.

- Introduction: This section explains why you undertook the project as well as what your premise or thesis was.
- Methods: This section is sometimes called materials and methods and conveys what you used to do the work as well as what was studied.
- Results: This sets out the findings of your work.
- Discussion: This section discusses what your work means and how it fits in with the existing body of literature. This section is sometimes called the summary or conclusion.

The format of the poster's content is sometimes mandated by the conference organizer. By using the standard format, the audience and readers can more clearly understand the work you did and your conclusions. Whether IMRaD or something else, following the format in your subject area is very important. Table 11.1 shows a sampling of how organizational structure within an article may vary by subject area. Seek out articles in your field to understand the common structures.

- References: Try to balance these citations. While it is best to keep your references in this tight format to the minimum, you also do not want to *not* cite something and therefore have someone accuse you of using someone else's ideas without attribution. If your reference list is long, include the bare minimum on the poster and then put the rest online and link to the full list. Another strategy is to list a shortened version of a reference with the DOI (digital object identifier) which is a unique and permanent web address assigned to online articles, books, and other works.
- Acknowledgments: These next three sections will conclude your poster. Acknowledgments may include any funders or organizations/ people that provided critical support. This is not where authors get to thank everyone in their lives; focus on the more critical players that made the work happen.
- Disclosure statements: Depending on your field or the organizer, you may need to list any conflicts of interest the authors might have. Other statements in this area might include ethics compliance or a

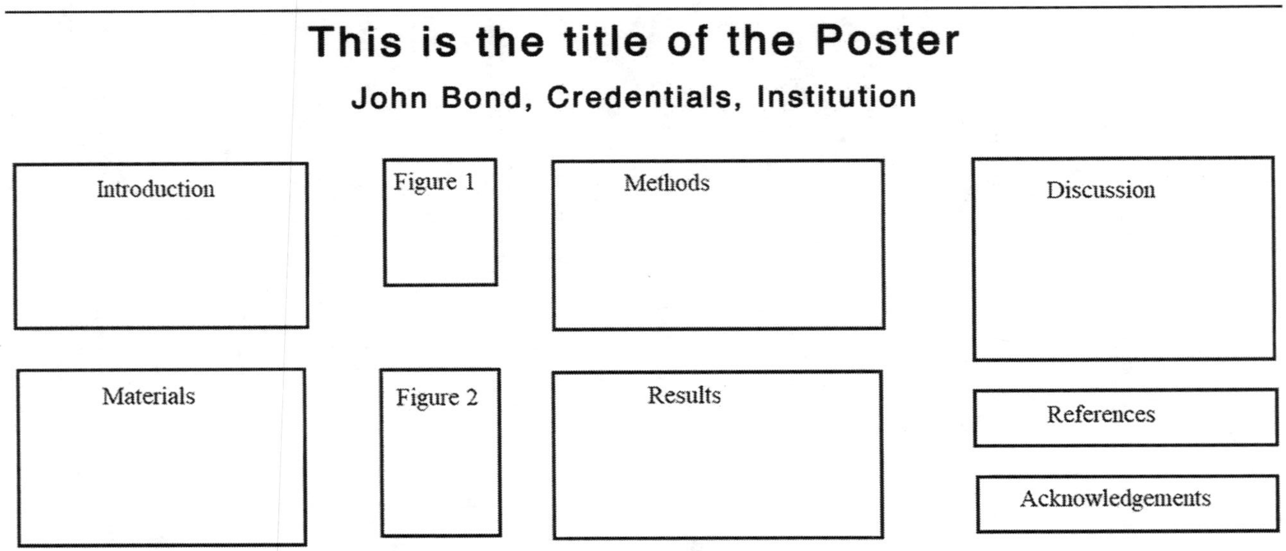

This is the title of the Poster

John Bond, Credentials, Institution

Introduction

Materials

Figure 1

Figure 2

Methods

Results

Discussion

References

Acknowledgements

Note: There are many items that you can add to your poster, and innumerable ways to arrnage it. This one is very generic and does not even scratch the surface.

Figure 11.2.   Sample Poster

statement about the diversity, equity, and inclusion regarding the subjects of the study or the authors.

- More information: You may wish to include ways to contact the presenters (emails, social media handles, etc.). You might also include a simplified web link or QR code for attendees to download your handout (more on that later) or to get your full reference list or supplemental data.

These are the main textual parts of a poster. See figure 11.2 for a sample layout of one poster. There are many possibilities. Pick the one that works best for you.

The graphic images (including figures, tables, and more) are discussed later in chapter 14. These elements can be the most crucial part of your poster, so do not overlook them.

Some people will dive into creating content or writing by using a program like PowerPoint. Others will use a word-processing program. No matter what works for you, seeing the steps in the process is important. So now let us move on to creating your content.

Chapter 12

Creating a Content Outline

Nothing is new except arrangement. —Will Durant

Start your work by creating an outline of the content that you will present. Use a traditional outline format. You will have to focus on the key points of your work. By their very nature, posters are concise, brief works. Likely what your project has involved is bigger than could be adequately summarized in a poster. That is what authoring a journal article is for, but that is down the road. Your outline will help you decide on what needs to be communicated and what does not.

This part of the process is more about content than actual content creation or writing. Think through the points that support your thesis and abstract. What are the essential facts the audience will need to know to understand your work?

New authors and presenters usually err on the side of including too much versus too little. They attempt to be comprehensive, which is good in most instances. However, when it comes to presenting your work in poster form, it can be counterproductive. Imagine that you have one gem of a finding or idea that you want to relay. You need to boil it down to the essence of that idea and then see what information supports it for the average person to appreciate (and agree with).

This focus on what is important will help you gain and keep the audience's attention.

This planning is unlike other scholarly communications that (mostly) have the luxury of space. A journal article encompasses an array of details; poster presentations do not. There are reasons to not go overboard when writing a manuscript for a peer-review journal article, but that is a different topic. Suffice it to say posters need to narrow the reader's attention quickly.

You can mark some of your ideas as primary (or must-haves) and others as secondary (or "would be nice to include"). When you start the actual writing process in the next chapter, you will use this outline as your guide to what will be included.

Let us look at the road ahead as a series of separate (but linked) tasks, such as creating the ideas (or words), noting your courses, and (most of all) creating eye-catching visuals.

So, first step—let us actually start writing!

Chapter 13

Writing Your First Draft

Words are all we have. —Samuel Beckett

The first step in drafting the text of your poster will be understanding any word count limits. Depending on the size of the poster, the word counts will vary. You may see suggestions for maximum counts of 500, 650, 800, 1,000, or other amounts. Conference organizers will probably not mandate a maximum word count, but they may make suggestions or link to articles or videos on optimal poster design and layout. Whatever target number you are going to use, stick to or be under it. This is a great exercise in being concise and focused.

To achieve this conciseness, use a certain assumed level of knowledge by your audience. It is a fine line between overexplaining basic concepts and assuming your audience is as deeply invested in your topic as you are. Straddling that line will help keep your work lean.

KISS or Keep It Simple Stupid is a principle to live by. Simplicity should be a key goal in writing and academic communication, and unnecessary complexity should be avoided at all costs. Sampling academic publishing would lead a reader to believe authors are trying for the exact opposite. Many articles or monographs can be long-winded and dense. But adhering to the KISS principle will take you far in your academic career. Simple writing is elegant.

Use your document format, IMRaD for example, as an overlay to the outline you created in the previous chapter. Now start to flesh out each section. Short sentences and short paragraphs are optimal in poster presentations. Best of all is text or concepts that can be explained in bullet or list form.

Walk the reader through your work and ideas in a process-oriented fashion. Your document format headings (abstract, introduction, methods, etc.) will help guide the reader.

Draft your entire poster before you concern yourself with images or tables. Editing will be covered in chapter 16, so get all the text written first.

Do not try to include the most complete explanations of complex ideas on a poster but do use text to convey key points and to announce that you have supplemental handouts.

Remember our discussion about your target audience. Keeping them in mind the whole time will help you hit the appropriate level—not too high or low.

Writers and authors should get in the habit of keeping all their drafts and notes and not overwriting or deleting them. In the age of (nearly) unlimited digital space, no one wants to regret deleting important information or what its source was. If you practice this, be aware of a strict file-naming system (document/version 1, version 2; or document version 10/13/2022, version 10/31/2022).

As you write your first draft, make sure you have captured the essence of your idea and findings. Have you covered all the salient points? Will the reader understand your process and agree with your conclusions?

A consideration for all writing, including academic writing, is the concept of storytelling. At first blush, this may seem a foreign idea. This is not a novel, you might say. But there has been a growing trend with successful scholarly authors to appreciate the importance of storytelling. We are human beings, and we all appreciate an engaging narrative, even if it is a technical one. Our brains are constantly trying to pull us away to something else: our phones, the next poster, lunch. When we listen to someone who uses storytelling, we become more engaged with the material We understand it better, care about it more. All of this translates into great feedback with the audience, greater recognition, and a brighter future in your academic writing and research career.

As you write your first draft, picture yourself explaining to a smart person what you did and what your conclusions were. Tell it with enthusiasm. Trying to draw the reader through from start to finish. You will benefit in the long run and so will your audience.

The mechanics of writing is the subject of countless other books and cannot be adequately summarized here. A few comments though: Be mindful of gender-neutral language. Make every effort to use language that is gender-inclusive in your work (e.g., chairperson as opposed to chairman). Tenses are important. There may be times when present and past tense are called for. Read other posters or work in your field to see the standards, noting different uses in different circumstances. For example: present tense will be used when discussing the work, you are presenting ("This poster takes astrophysics as an example of . . ."). The past tense will be used when discussing experiments that have occurred in the past or works previously done by cited authors ("Smith has previously examined . . ."). Finally, use active versus passive voice. Most novice writers struggle with identifying active and passive voice. Passive sounds detached whereas active sounds action-oriented. There are times when either active or passive voice is appropriate in academic writing.

In the "Bibliography" section of the book is a list of some great works on writing to help with the mechanics, but do not let the challenge of this area intimidate you or keep you from participating. With the little free time in your day, consider one of these to help long term with your writing.

See chapter 16 for a discussion on what programs you might want to consider, whether you are interested in a basic word-processing program or something a bit more robust.

Now you have your first draft. Before you edit and share your work, there are two other important tasks to discuss.

Chapter 14

Deciding on What Information to Express Visually

It is like icing on the cake. —Anonymous

The audience engages with physical poster presentations on a real-time basis. Many (but not all) attendees at poster sessions will stroll by and casually glance at a poster (and the presenter) and make a snap decision whether to stop and experience it. At large conferences, most people do not have the time (or interest) to dive into every poster. People curate the session by looking for topics that resonate with or intrigue them. But part of the curation is a snap decision by glancing at the poster. First, they look at the title to determine the topic, but the next thing they do (almost at the same time) is scan the poster for visuals. The mind likes visuals (as opposed to a poster of all text).

Your challenge is to decide what information from your work should be expressed in visual format. Images, figures, photos, and tables will draw a reader's attention as they pass by. Knowing this may lead a novice author to jam their presentation full of visuals and reduce or eliminate text. Almost all visuals are probably a better choice than all text, but this is not the answer to a successful poster.

The key is choosing the most essential information that can be expressed in visual format. You want the reader or viewer to look at your title and then the visuals and *instantly* understand where you are going with your work and your conclusions.

Of course, not all visuals are the same. Some visuals are tables. Tables many times will show your results but might also show other key data points. If you choose to show tables, select those with greatest impact and highlight the salient points. Tabular material should not be repeated in the text.

Some visuals are photographs. This is especially true in science and in medicine (in case reports). Make sure any images being shown are high quality and show at a glance the essence of your work. If the photo is a clinical one, never alter the image. Also, keep the same ratio when you increase or decrease it in size so there is no proportional distortion.

Finally, some visuals are charts such as bar or pie charts, line graphs, histograms, Venn diagrams, infographics, and others. These types of visuals can have great impact. Using bold or color in these types of images can help focus a reader's attention. More on this in chapter 22.

A valuable piece of writing advice is to "show not say." This is an important guideline for writing, and certainly applies to poster presentations. But once again, how do you strike the balance with the right number and type of visuals?

Look through the draft of your work. What content could have the greatest impact on the reader? You are looking for information that best explains your results and conclusions. Make a list of possible visuals to accompany your work. List as many as possible. Maybe some can explain your materials/methods or the population you looked at?

Then prioritize them for value. Which ones will cut to the heart of your work? Some will gravitate to the top of your list, and others to the bottom. This will allow you to make some decisions. There is an optimal number of visuals for any given poster, and that is exactly which ones will catch and keep the reader's attention.

It would be nice to say the number is five or eight, but that cannot be done. The size of the poster, your topic, and your subject matter makes an exact number impossible to determine. Suffice to say zero or one is *likely* too few. Twenty or more is *likely* too many. What your target number is will be up to you. In chapter 18, we will discuss getting feedback from potential readers. After you determine your best amount and create them, you may wish to ask your readers if you chose correctly. If you are on the fence, err on the side of fewer. You can add them later.

Another inclination with new authors is to combine data points from a few images into one, in an effort to have fewer but more impactful figures. This might be the way to go, but tread lightly. Complex and difficult-to-digest charts can be worse than too many. The best situation is if a reader can look at the title of the graphic, then at the x and y axis and then say, "Wow, look at what they found."

Once you have made your list, you may need to revise or change your first draft of the text. Make these changes but remember to keep your original version in case you change your mind!

Finally, all of these recommendations were focused on a physical poster. Of course, your presentation may be an ePoster, or perhaps it is both digital and physical. Many of the suggestions above will still apply in the digital realm. The one major difference will be the quick scan of the whole work. This will obviously not occur in the same way, but viewers will still evaluate each graphic for how well it can be understood and what it quickly conveys.

Now you have your adjusted first draft and list of visuals. More information will be offered in chapter 22 on how to create these visuals from a software point-of-view.

A side note: each figure and table need to be cited in the presentation's text, such as Table 1, Table 2, Figure 1, Figure 2. Figures and tables are numbered separately. Tables have headings, and figures have captions. Some word-processing programs do not make a distinction between figures and tables, giving both of them captions. Make sure the heading or the caption is complete in case they appear separate from the presentation. For other formatting, such as capitalizing words in the table title and more, see the style manual you have been using.

Be aware that in some fields (e.g., the sciences), choosing images is the first step in the process. Sage advice in these areas has been, "Pick the images that best convey your results, then write the text that supports them."

Also, some authors have started the whole process with one eye-catching figure and built the rest of the work around it. This is okay if you have figure(s) that will grab a person's attention.

Be sure to clearly convey what prior work got you to where you are so others can understand where you are coming from.

Chapter 15

Keeping Track of Your Sources and References

A good decision is based on knowledge . . . —Plato

All scholarly communication is standing on the shoulders of giants. Poster presentations are no exception. Your work builds on an enormous body of literature in your field and your specific topic. You probably have done a wide-ranging literature search as part of your larger project or work. If not, well there is no time like the present to rectify the situation.

Literature searches are critical steps in all academic communication. There are separate educational resources on doing a literature review, including books, websites, videos, and more. If you feel new to the area or insecure about your skills, seek out dedicated resources on this. A key piece of advice from many scholarly authors is to develop a close connection with a research librarian at your institution. They can help maximize your efforts and minimize your time.

Let us assume that you have done a literature review connected to your poster presentation. You have (perhaps) a lengthy list of references that will place your work in context. Deciding on what references to include is an important decision. Astute readers will look for the essential references connected to your work. Of the work you choose to cite on the actual poster, ensure that they are the critical ones and cited properly.

There is a fine line to walk with references between too few and too many. Include the classic references in your field and those that directly support your work. Do not turn your reference section into a bibliography of all the works published on the topic.

Another consideration is giving proper credit to your sources and influences. Keeping track of and properly citing the literature connected with your topic is critical. Plagiarism is an ugly word that can follow a writer or researcher for years, even when its use is unfair or unfounded. Of course, there are the rare few who intentionally take whole tracts of text from others without giving credit. They are in large part the exceptions. Most "plagiarism" accusations are more connected with the author not properly citing a source. As you pull together those references related to your work, be mindful of leaving no question as to the ground on which your work is built.

Many times, presenters will realize they need a lengthier list than the poster may allow. They may list a few and then offer a QR code, web address, or handout to give the complete list. Poster presentations do not have the luxury of the long reference list that journal articles normally have. But the references they do list should be essential. You may choose to have only a few on the poster and the rest somewhere else, but you must include the full list. Check with the conference organizers to verify whether the alternative listing idea (websites, handouts, etc.) fits within their guidelines.

Keep track of any resource you refer to during your work. There is some great bibliographic management software (such as EndNote, Mendeley, etc.). A list is included in the "Resources" section in this book. The sooner you adopt one of these tools, the easier your life will become.

A side note: strive to have all content in your presentation be original. Having material (a table, an image, some text) from a third party (such as a peer-review journal or monograph) will mean you must seek permission from the owner or publisher of that material. The process can slow down your efforts and there may be a fee (possibly a hefty one) to use the material. There certainly are some instances when you will need specific content from a source but try to minimize these. If you need to seek permission, start early. Also, never rely on the concept of fair use for any image, table, or long tract of text. "Grabbing something off a website" is never an acceptable strategy. When in doubt, cite the material and seek permission.

Compiling references may not be the most exciting part of your academic communications journey, but it is an essential step and one that needs to be done thoroughly.

Chapter 16

Editing Your Draft

Ask yourself at every moment, "Is this necessary?"
—*Marcus Aurelius*

You have your first draft, and your references are all set. You have chosen which information will be displayed graphically. Now, it is time to ensure that you have as close to a final draft with as clear and concise writing as possible.

Editing need not be an onerous or anxiety-producing task. Here are the key points to turn your first draft into a tightly edited final draft:

- Editing may mean rewriting. It would be great if your first draft just needed some small tweaks; however, be open to the possibility of rewriting sections that are unclear or not up to par.
- Everyone involved needs to read it. All coauthors or parties involved need to read through the draft and give feedback with potential comments to the lead author or designated contact. This person will take all the feedback and produce a new draft for everyone to review again. No one who has their name on the poster should be excused from the editing and feedback stage of the process.
- Reduce jargon. Inevitably, jargon creeps into almost all academic work. Try to assiduously avoid it. Think about the cross-disciplinary readers of your work. They may not be as deeply invested in the terminology. Likewise, spell out all abbreviations and acronyms at first mention.

- Closely review the abstract or introduction. These may be the only parts of your work that someone might get to as they decide if the poster interests them.
- It may take more than one round of edits. Skimping on editing benefits no one. Be patient.
- Run a spelling and grammar check. It seems like a simple idea but utilize the power of your word-processing software's review option. It can help more than people believe.
- Read it aloud. My top suggestion to authors is to read your work aloud several times. The ear and the tongue can identify many places that your work needs some attention. Listen to your brain about any concerns with torturous sentence construction or ambiguity. Read the work aloud as the work progresses through several iterations. Alternatively, most word-processing software now includes a read-aloud function. This feature has become remarkably sophisticated. Please use it.
- As you embark on your writing career, you might want to consider what software you are using. Microsoft Word and Apple Pages are fine programs that can get the job done. Using other writing software programs has become popular. Programs such as Evernote, Grammarly, and others have gained devoted fans. Many of these programs offer dedicated writing tools and have integrated bibliographic management aspects to them. A list of both writing and authoring programs and bibliographic management software are noted in the "Resources" section at the end of the book. Also, there are document preparation systems. One system is called LaTeX. There are others. These systems are valuable for power users and can offer benefits Word does not. For academics or researchers new to writing and publishing, stick to a basic word-processing program like Word or a bibliographic management system like EndNote. When you are new to the process, getting words on the page is the most important part. Learning complicated systems like LaTeX while you are crafting one of your first articles simply slows you down.
- As mentioned in the previous chapter, unintended plagiaristic issues can cause big problems. Run your manuscript through plagiarism-checking software. This software does not guarantee that there is not an issue, but it can point toward any concerns. A web search will list a range of options for plagiarism-checking software. Sometimes your

authoring software (such as Grammarly) will offer this option. It may be built in or available as a plug-in for an additional fee. If you work at a university, your library or department may subscribe to one of several services. Check with them. Do not skip this step before finalizing your poster.

Endeavor to make the text of your poster clear and concise. Your efforts through the editing process will pay off with greater interest, more citations, and increased visibility.

Chapter 17

Following a Style Manual

In character, in manner, in style, in all things, the supreme excellence is simplicity. —Henry Wadsworth Longfellow

In the process of creating your poster, you will have decisions to make. Can I have too few or too many words? How big or small should my font be? When I use the abbreviation "e.g.," should I use periods after it or not? What form should my references be in?

As you progress in your academic authoring career, understanding the helpful tools that are at your disposal is important. They save time and they help avoid mistakes.

The conference organizer will likely give instructions on what form your poster presentation should take. These guidelines can vary widely. Some give concrete instructions, others may refer to a third party for advice, and some may say little other than basic information such as the size of the poster. Find out where this is listed. It may be in the original call for poster presentations, at the conference website, in your invitation/acceptance email or notice, or other places. If you cannot find this, email the organizer and ask for access to their instructions.

This information could be informal (poster size, number of words, major categories such as IMRaD to use), they may be more detailed, or they may refer to helpful documents with all sorts of guidance and advice. Sometimes they link to videos that cover some of the information presented in this book.

However extensive and whatever the format, follow it closely and do not deviate. If the organizers prefer the references in APA format versus AMA format, follow it to the letter. Most conferences will use judges or a committee to review your poster on-site. One of the criteria that they may use is adherence to standards or formats, with style manuals and conference guidelines being just one aspect. Some conferences may use, "Follow designated format?" as one of many criteria to compare your work to the others. You do not want to "lose" points for such a straightforward task. Read the instructions, and then read them again.

The conference organizer may also designate a style manual or style guide that they prefer. It is likely the one in use in your field. A style manual is a set of standards for writing and designing specific documents such as journal articles.

Style manuals may be specific to a subject area. They can be extremely detailed and very specific. They run several hundred pages and give detailed information on such things as reference formatting, footnoting, table formation, and many other seemingly minute areas.

Style manuals can be valuable to beginning writers, as well as veterans. The correct use of one quickly illustrates whether authors are novice or veteran writers. They highlight the importance of consistency of style within a document. They show the author's ability to see their work as a whole rather than a collection of individual parts. Of course, professor should be capitalized when attached to a last name, such as Professor Bond. But when the word appears by itself in the text, should professor be capitalized? A style manual will surely weigh in on these and thousands of other details. They also serve as a refresher course for many areas of language that remain elusive to authors.

There are some very well-known style manuals. Here are a few:

- *AMA Manual of Style: A Guide for Authors and Editors*
- *The Chicago Manual of Style*
- *MLA Handbook*
- *Publication Manual of the American Psychological Association*

There are others. A list is included in the resources in this book. Likely at this point you know the style manual that is preferred in your subject area. Read and follow it closely, but any guidance the conference organizer gives about the format of your poster presentation supersedes the manual.

These practices (using a style manual and reviewing the communication partner's instructions) is a great habit to get in for the rest of your academic career. These tasks are time-consuming but you need to conform to the expectations of your readers. You will have a greater connection to the attendees as well as an increased chance of acceptance in future academic endeavors.

Now, let us get some feedback on your work.

Chapter 18

Getting Feedback from Colleagues and Reviewers

Examine what is said and not who speaks. —*Proverb*

You have the content of your poster presentation written. You have your final formatted reference list. The text has been edited, and you have checked it compared to your chosen style manual and instructions from the conference organizer. All set? Not yet.

One last recommendation is to share your work with colleagues to get comments and feedback. This may be done at this stage, or you may wish to do this earlier in the process. Do not send your work out for comment before it is edited because your reviewers might mistake small errors in format for sloppiness in writing or researching.

You will need to give your colleagues or the reviewers a specific charge regarding what feedback you want: Comments on your writing? Your conclusions? Or everything? Give them permission to be honest. Tell them you want truthful feedback, pro and con. This may cause you some anxiety, but you need to hear diverse opinions before you consider your work ready for the next steps. Be sure to provide them with the proposal submission guidelines and name the specific conference in the case they have previously attended and have familiarity with their criteria.

If you can get feedback from several colleagues, put their comments into perspective. Of course, if they note a misspelled word or a technical problem that is black and white, make the change. Many times, however, the feedback is subjective.

Reviewers are commenting on their vision of your work. Carefully consider all comments in a constructive manner, even if they were not delivered that way. Try not to be defensive. Consider whether you agree with the comments, and if your work would be improved by a change that addresses their idea. Perhaps their comment does not represent your vision for the work—in that case, pass on making that change. Review is not meant as personal validation. Instead, it is a way for you to create the best possible work to display as a poster and garner the most interest. If a reviewer seems to misunderstand what you wrote, rather than dismissing the comment, consider whether this is a signal as to how your current work could be misunderstood and how you could be clearer in presenting your point.

When considering feedback, look for themes across all the reviews, such as the writing, if the concepts are too simple or complex, if it needs more substance, etc. Give these themes the greatest weight and credence. Also, remember to thank anyone who takes the time to offer advice. Offer to give them feedback on any of their future research or writing. This is how you build a valuable network of like-minded, helpful writers.

Sometimes the challenge is getting colleagues who have the time and expertise to review your work. Often a supervisor or a coworker will assist you. You might also ask acquaintances from your university days or someone you have worked with in the past on other projects.

Looking beyond your list of contacts, you may wish to seek out other experts to give you feedback. One approach is asking your colleagues for suggestions of reviewers. Looking toward people who have published or presented at meetings in your topic area can provide other possibilities. A general web search can yield potentials. Academic social network sites like Academia.edu, ResearchGate, and others are valuable tools to find reviewers. If you are unfamiliar with these sites, check them out and sign up for an account.

If your material is heavily dependent on statistics, consider getting a review by someone qualified in statistics. This may be difficult, but you will want to ensure your work is built on a sound foundation.

Some authors are concerned about giving people unknown to them an advanced peek into the work they are doing. Others are concerned about the time it takes to add this step into the process and the associated delay. Some may limit the number of people to share their work with by choosing only the most reliable and timely reviewers.

Your goal is to present the best possible poster at the conference. Having your work in its optimal form will put you in the best light.

Feedback (and validation) are important steps in your academic authoring career. Use this practice in all your efforts. Sometimes you may want to implement it earlier in the process and sometimes later. No matter when, use this practice to your advantage.

Now, take one more check of your work. Consider running a spelling and grammar check again. Read it aloud one more time. Rereview the instructions from the conference organizer. Now it's time to move on to design and layout.

Part IV

CREATING THE POSTER

Chapter 19

Getting Started

The secret of getting ahead is getting started. —Mark Twain

As you move from writing and content creation to layout and design, there are some factors you have to consider.

First is who will actually do the work. There are several options.

- Some institutions or universities have departments or people specifically charged with helping authors or researchers craft and create their academic communications. These are highly trained graphic artists and/or editors. This option will greatly simplify your life and make your effort so much more attractive. If this option is open to you, it is best to proceed this way.
- You can create the materials yourself using sophisticated programs to do the poster layout. Software such as Adobe InDesign, Illustrator, and Photoshop are powerful tools that create a presentation that would rival any designer's work. The drawbacks here are several. The software comes at a fee. The good news is, for many of these higher-end products, you can subscribe to them for a month or two. Or you may have a subscription through your institution. Another point to consider is that they all have a learning curve. Yes, they are intuitive and come with great training videos. But your time is limited, and your main focus is writing and research, not design. Also, your skill set may not include the creativity a frequent user of the software might bring to it.

- You can use a more accessible program to create the poster layout. Software from Microsoft (PowerPoint, Publisher), Apple (Pages, Keynote), or Google (Docs, Slides) can also produce elegant and well-crafted poster presentations. But the concern here is that these programs are underused, and the poster ends up likely simplistic or amateurish. If you go down this road, ensure you are harnessing all of the potential of these programs.
- For digital posters in some fields, certain conference organizers use vendors who provide or offer their own layout and design software ("iPosterSessions," 2022).
- The final option is to hire a freelance graphic artist to create your work. It is easier and simpler than you might imagine. Websites like Fiverr, Upwork, Freelancer, and others allow you to effortlessly connect with experienced individuals (locally and around the world) to design your poster. Two pieces of advice if you go this route: Do not simply choose the least-expensive person. You get what you pay for. Also, when choosing between possible freelancers, look toward the number of times they have done similar work and their ratings. Pick a good one.

A point to consider no matter which option you choose—your poster is about your ideas and conclusions. You have been chosen (or hope to be chosen) because of your subject-matter expertise, not for your graphic-arts ability. Balance this point with the opposite problem (great content, poor presentation). Strike a balance between paying enough attention to presentation and too little.

If you choose either of the "do-it-yourself" options above, be aware that there are some great templates for poster creation. Some are basic but others are more complex and versatile. A quick web search will show lots of templates as well, some from third parties. A few are freely available for use. One of the challenges with web search is the confusion between academic poster presentations and a poster to be hung on a wall. Double-check any results (for a freelancer or template) that you have the right type of poster! If you end up using your institution for creation, they will surely be starting from a template that resonates with you.

The second factor to consider is the different details involved if your work will be a paper poster, a digital poster, or both. Many conferences (pre-COVID) still did paper poster presentations despite being twenty-five years into the digital era. This made and still makes sense. When there is a live event, in-person posters are a better experience for both the presenter and the audience member. The give-and-take can add richness and depth to the conversation. But the paper poster is limited to those people who wander by. When executed optimally by the organizer, ePosters can have a long reach. At this point of the process, ensure you understand which you are responsible for creating. If the answer is both, does one file suffice for both or do you need to offer the same content in multiple file or presentation formats?

No matter which, find the exact specifications for the presentation(s). These will likely be in the information from the organizer. Dive in and ensure you understand what they expect. If you have any questions, make sure you get all of them answered.

Digital posters can be displayed on large monitors, which allows for features such as videos, animations, narrations, and other resources. Of course, some presenters can overdo the glitz of videos, audio, music, and more. But when properly used, they can be powerful additions to the work.

Collections of ePosters can be viewed at the conference on desktop monitors. They also provide a means for conference organizers to create digital archives of current and past poster sessions. Some sites offer ePosters for all to see under an open-access philosophy (open access allows unlimited use to anyone with internet access, and places few to no restrictions on the reuse of the content with proper citation) ("ePosters," 2022). Some organizations have been able to include question-and-answer sessions with digital posters and even to archive them.

Whether paper or digital, make sure you fully understand what the expectations are. Have all the specifications at hand and if there are any questions, make sure to ask the organizer. Now, let us dive into the actual layout.

Chapter 20

Understanding Text Sizes, Layout, and More

It's not what you look at that matters, it's what you see.
—*Henry David Thoreau*

Now you will dive into the actual tasks of transforming your words and ideas into a graphic, pleasing, visual presentation. As you work your way to this point, try to think about the posters you have seen prior to this. What caught your eye? What did not work? Become a connoisseur of other poster presentations, both from a content point of view but also from the visual aspect.

Remember that your starting point is to follow the instructions from the conference organizer. Begin with these. Ask questions on what is unclear or about anything that you do not understand. After that, it comes down to your opinions on what is aesthetically pleasing.

Here is a list of factors to think about or consider as you compose the actual poster:

• Will the poster be vertical or horizontal in its orientation?
• What is the size of the poster? Common sizes are 4 by 6 feet or 4 by 8 feet (or 1 by 3 or 4 meters), but they can vary.
• How many columns will you use for the presentation? Three or four columns is common. You want the content to be readable so set column widths so readers do not lose their place or become fatigued as their eyes move across the section. A column width of ten inches is a good starting guide. There are occasions when two or even five

columns might work; usually this is determined by the size and orientation of the poster. Also consider the border around the entire content. It may be tempting to push it to the limit and move the text close to the edge. White space will be discussed in the next chapter. Use consistent (and maybe even generous) margins around the edges and between columns. It will ease the reader's eyes if they do not have to absorb densely packed materials. The outer border or margin on full-size posters should be at least two to three inches.

- Some authors put each block of text or section (introduction, methods, etc.) in a box to show the reader the extent of that part. After you decide if you would like to use boxes or not, consider how the reader will move from section to section. Will they read all the way down column one and then jump back up to the top of column two? Or will they read all the way across the first row and then jump to the second row? (See figure 11.1 in chapter 11 for an example of the two methods of content flow.) In most instances, authors choose to have readers go all the way down column one and then jump back up to column two. This may seem counterintuitive since most cultures in the Western world read left to right, then move to the next line. If you feel your layout may confuse the reader, you can always use arrows to show them where to go after they read a section. Another method to show the order of your material is to number each section.

How the blocks of text are aligned is another factor. Justified or flush left (or ragged right) are the only two real options. There are strong cases to be made for both. A factor to consider is that academic writing and publishing many times contains long, technical words. If you use justified margins, these long words can lead to some lines being oddly spaced. Therefore, using flush left body text may present the best choice.

An option is to include a block of text, which might be a single key passage or quote. These are sometimes referred to as a callout, pull quote, lift quote, or other. This single quote could summarize the work or its implication, it may position it in the field, it may present a startling statistic, or more. You are probably most accustomed to seeing these in a magazine article. Use one of these quotes only if there is a single, brief, textual point that can make a significant impact on the reader that cannot be made in a graphic.

- Next will be your font choice. This may seem like an easy decision but give it some more thought. Choose run-of-the-mill fonts such as Helvetica or Times New Roman. The first is a sans serif font and the second a serif font. A serif refers to the short lines stemming from or at an angle to the upper and lower tips of the stroke of a letter. Sans serif (without serifs) are boxier. Serifs have more flourish. Whatever font you choose, pick common or familiar ones—no gimmicky fonts. Old English or Comic Sans may seem fun or quirky, but they quickly lose their novelty as the reader may tire of deciphering what they say. It is not uncommon to use two different fonts in the poster. A sans serif font like Helvetica might be used in the title, the figure captions, and tables. A serif font like Times New Roman might be used in the body text and in the references.

  Many fonts will have a family to choose from such as condensed, demi, medium, light, and more. The condensed options are usually better for the title while the traditional version will work better for the body text. All your choices should be driven by readability. Also, some authors love to use bold, underline, or italic to make a point. Your concepts should make the statement for you, not bolding a word. Of course, there are proper times to use underline and italic in the references list and the like. Other authors may employ punctuation to make a point such as an exclamation point or gimmicks such as all capital letters. Don't do THIS! Generally, do not use text in all uppercase or capital letters. Perhaps you can display the title this way, but do not use all uppercase for any significant length of text. If you use extensive special characters (Greek letters, math symbols, etc.), look at how your chosen font presents these characters.

- Next is type size. Remember the word count range discussed in chapter 13 (500, 650, 800, 1,000, or other amounts). When deciding the appropriate type size, readability at a distance is the key factor. You may wish to reconsider how much text you have included and pare back in favor of a larger font and more readability. Conversely, if you find the text size that works for you and have extra space, consider whether you were too harsh in cutting material and whether you can include additional critical content. Most readers of a paper poster will be standing about four to six feet away when they are scanning your material to see if it is of interest to them. To understand what the implications of type size are, print out a series of headlines and text on a test sheet of printer paper and read it from a distance.

Suggested type sizes vary and there is no one standard (Block, 1996). Titles may range from 120 point to 85 with 100 being a good starting point. Body text may range from 48 point to 24 with 28 being a good starting point. The following page has some examples of the type of text you might find in a paper poster presentation with possible suggested type sizes (in actual font size). Listed as well are some of the items you will use on a poster presentation (title, text, table, and figure text) and some possible point sizes (pts) to consider. Two sample fonts are used Times New Roman (TNR) and Helvetica (Hv). All of these are changeable depending on the size of your poster, subject matter, your preferences, and many more items.

Deciding on type size may be a work in progress. Your poster is a delicate balance between the all-important content, readability, type size, and space. The decisions with one (adding extra text in or the complete reference list) has impacts on the others. Likewise, making the type size very small or very large has a great impact on a poster.

Consider also the spacing in your font. It could be single, double, or other spacing. This greatly affects readability at a distance. Play with spacing when you do your test printing. For body text, double spacing is most commonly chosen. For references, single spacing within the reference and then an extra space between the references is common. As previously discussed, your poster has to be a balance between the amount of text and the number of quality, engaging graphics/images. As you decide on type size, you will need to think carefully about the decisions you made regarding the number of images. See the next chapter for actually creating your visuals.

• When you have laid out your poster, try to look at it with fresh eyes. Whenever a person looks at something, their eye likely goes somewhere first. It may be due to color, boldness, size, position, balance, or other factors. Many times, the eye will be drawn to the right place (or the intended location), but other times it may not be. If your eye is not drawn to the most important spots, rearrange the poster's layout or change an item position to help the reader follow your story. Also, the eye will likely impose or imagine a flow to the work (and it may not be as intended). Sometimes enlisting friends or colleagues to take a quick glance at your work for the first time, may be the best way to understand the flow and balance of the poster.

Title 100 pts Hv bold

Subtitle 50 pts Hv

Author names/ affiliations 36 pts Hv

Primary head 36 pts TNR

Secondary head 30 pts TNR

Body text 24 TNR

References 16 pts TNR

Figure caption 20 pts Hv bold

Table title 20 pts Hv bold

Table column header 16 pts Hv bold

Table column data 14 pts Hv

Acknowledgments, conflict-of-interest disclosures, and other ending material points 14 pts TNR

Do these guidelines apply if your poster is paper, digital, or both? Many of the concepts discussed above still apply, while others matter less or not at all. Your choice of font is still important while the readability at a distance is slightly less relevant to a digital presentation. Securing the file format and specifications will help tease out which points need to be addressed, adapted, or dropped.

For digital presentations, your images may need to be modified or saved in an alternate format. Images can vary in resolution, usually expressed in dpi or dots per inch. When reproducing an image for printing, consider 300 dpi. Be careful when enlarging any image simply by resizing it. When using images only for ePosters, a lower dpi such as 150 or 72 is more than acceptable and it will help make your file load faster.

For those digital poster presentations that allow video and animation, follow file specifications carefully while trying to present the highest-quality material possible. Consider adding music as long as it does not distract from your presentation.

Another tack that some have taken is to connect with experienced presenters and have them guide you, probably by "lending" you their template. It can be effective—and after several times presenting, you will be the lender.

There are a lot of details to work through in this chapter. Consider reading the chapter twice, making notes the second time around of items for you to address. Design and layout are important but, at the end of the day, your work and your words/visuals are what will resonate with audience members. Your ideas will further your academic writing and publishing career. The design and layout simply allow readers to experience your idea in a pleasing, unencumbered manner.

Chapter 21

Using Whitespace and Color

Colors, like features, follow the changes of the emotions.
—Pablo Picasso

How your poster looks at a glance, whether you think it is fair or not, matters. Conference attendees and other audience members for poster presentations are bombarded with information, advertisements, and distractions during their entire day. When they are engaging with posters, they want to focus quickly on the topic and key message. Many of the suggestions in this book are geared toward increasing the chance of engaging the reader.

In the previous chapter, several topics focused on the overall visual layout to allow for maximum readability. Let us look at two more.

Whitespace is very important. This area is more than the borders of the poster. It is the space between columns, space between lines of text, space in charts and tables, etc. A reader can look at a poster and see if the material they are viewing is dense and therefore difficult to follow or consume. Conversely, the reader may sense too much space and feel there is not enough there. Both of these evaluations may even be subconscious on behalf of the reader. But they are still there.

As the author, keep this in mind when making the many visual decisions ahead of you, specifically for paper presentations. Step back at various junctures and view your work as the viewer would. This is where printing out samples and standing back a few feet will give you an opportunity to experience what the reader sees. Look for places where your eye wanders and find ways to engage the viewer with space, a figure or image, color, or perhaps an arrow.

Color is another important way to engage readers. This, like white space, can help or hinder your efforts to capture eyeballs. A lack of color can make your presentation seem flat and dull, while too many or clashing colors can be a turnoff.

Colors will be of greatest use in items such as the title and subtitle, table headers, charts and graphs, and design elements. Experiment with various color combinations to see which ones work best. Some color combinations will not work on top of each other. Overlay bold, yellow text on top of a field of white and the text nearly disappears. Some striking combinations can be royal blue and yellow, red and black, green and blue, and more. Check with a colleague or friend to ensure your choice works for others.

Information regarding color choices for charts and graphs could fill a whole chapter or even a book (and likely does). Being able to easily follow the line(s) connecting data points on a graph is essential. Whether done with bold or color, help your reader's eye follow your line of thinking. The selective use of color in charts can also be very powerful. Making just the arrow in color, or certain bars in a chart in color can be extremely helpful in guiding the viewer to the salient points.

White text on a field of color (sometimes called reversed out) can be powerful, but it needs to be used judiciously. Some have tried whole posters with white text on a full-color background, but this can be fatiguing to the eye to read.

As the world moves toward being more inclusive, consider those individuals who have challenges with certain colors. People who are color vision deficient (or color blind) can find certain color combinations to be a challenge. A red/green deficiency can mean pie charts lose meaning when authors choose these colors. There are plenty of options in such cases for indicating sections of a chart such as solid, cross hatching, or numbering with a corresponding legend. Do not make your figures drab for this reason; rather, show your color choices to an array of people and ask about the readability of any complex charts or graphs.

These concepts apply with ePosters in some ways but less in others. Some computer programs are moving toward optional dark/night mode with inverted colors. Experiment with these settings to understand what your readers or viewers will be experiencing.

Some authors choose to use their institutional colors as their color guide. Loyalty is a good trait and branding is a powerful tool, but not all school colors are optimal or engaging. Choose for the reader, not your brand. Of course, your institution may add gravitas to your presentation. Harvard, CERN, and the United Nations are all high-power affiliations to brag about, but many times it is their reputation in your field that is key. Tread lightly.

When properly used, white space and color will engage and keep a reader and help ease them through complicated concepts. When done wrong, it can stop interest before the reader even knows the topic.

Chapter 22

Creating Eye-Catching Visuals

The true art of memory is the art of attention. Samuel Johnson

You have the text of your poster written and a preliminary layout. For the visuals, make sure you are presenting your most important elements in the best way possible. Assuming you are not working with a free-lance designer or professional to create your material, here are some points that may assist you in creating eye-catching visuals.

- First is what software to use when creating. Most laptops or desktop computers have powerful programs to create acceptable visuals. Microsoft offers Excel (for the tabular material), PowerPoint, and Word which have more capability than most people use. They also offer Visio and Publisher. Apple offers Numbers, Pages, Keynote, and iMovie. Google offers Docs, Sheets, Slides, and more. Before you pursue higher-powered programs, make sure you have exhausted what is likely available to you today at no fee. A list is included in the resources in this book.

   Stepping up to the higher level of programs to create great visuals, consider the Adobe Suite first. The programs Illustrator, Photoshop, and InDesign will likely present as much creative power as you need. These programs can be costly, but you may have access to them through your institution, or see if a month-by-month subscription service suits you. Adobe also offers a more affordable version of Photoshop called Photoshop Elements that does not have as many features but is really what many nonprofessionals need for basic tasks. Inkscape and GIMP are good free alternatives to Illustrator and Photoshop, respectively.

There are many other high-quality programs to create visuals, some with specific functions such as plotting, math-specific calculations, infographics, and others. A few are listed here but an internet search will offer many more. A short list to check out includes: Canva (graphic design platform), GraphPad Prism (analysis and graphing solution), MATLAB (plotting functions and data, implementation of algorithms), Mind the Graph (infographic creator), Origin (data analysis and graphing software), SigmaPlot (scientific graphing and data analysis), and many more.

Learning these programs can be time-consuming and a distraction, which might be an argument for working with a graphic artist. Most of the programs are fairly intuitive for basic use (Bond, 2023).

Review the conference guidelines to see if they address figure or table formatting. Also, review whatever style manual you have chosen to ensure compliance with formatting.

- Keep it simple. Do not overdesign the visuals. Readers want to be able to get to the heart of what is being discussed.
- Do not repeat information. Tables and figures should be the place where you present the data. Do not repeat the data from the text in a table or vice versa.
- There are other ways to present data besides a standard, two-column table. Bar graphs, line graphs, pie charts, scatterplot charts, and Venn diagrams are just a few examples. Get creative and consider flowcharts (to show your work), timelines (for your topic), or algorithms. The more visual your data is, the more likely it will engage the reader.
- Photographs can be an essential part of posters in certain fields. High-quality images can grab the reader's attention. Use fewer images to have greater impact unless you are showing a progression or process.
- Consider an infographic, if applicable. An infographic is a graphic visual representation of information, data, or knowledge intended to present information quickly and clearly. When done right, an infographic can be a magnet to any reader passing by your presentation. There is some separate software that has been championed to create them as well.

- Three-dimensional figures can be very striking when done well. Consider if any data or image can add to the poster. There are some specific programs available to create quality images. Only consider using this format if it adds to the reader's knowledge, as opposed to being a gimmick. If you do use multidimensional images, test ahead of time to see how they will be printed or rendered. No one wants the surprise of a flat, dull image plopped in the middle of the poster.
- While images are being discussed, consider adding a photo of the authors next to their names. It should be a head shot, nicely done, recent, and maybe even with a smile. It can add a personal touch, considering there may be times when the poster is available for viewing and you are not present.
- The previous chapter discussed the beneficial use of color and white space. These concepts are most important with your visuals in our 140-character, short-attention-span society. Experiment with both for readability and engagement.
- Whatever type of image you decide to use, make sure you see it printed out at the reproduction size to ensure it does not pixelate and become blurry and therefore diminished.

The saying that a picture is worth a thousand words applies most to the visuals for your presentation. Spend the time and energy to make them the centerpiece of your work.

Chapter 23

Your Final Draft and Final Review

Once we accept our limits, we go beyond them. —Albert Einstein

You are almost at the finish line. You have written and edited the content of your poster presentation. You have done the layout and graphic design. You now are ready to proceed, right? Let us pause and make one final check.

- Run one final spelling and grammar check on your text, tables, and figures. Better safe than sorry.
- Read it aloud one more time to ensure no awkward phrasing has crept in.
- Run your final work through any plagiarism-checking software you may have used. Confirm that your sources were cited and all ideas are given proper credit.
- Confirm that all materials are original. If you needed to seek permission, has the final paperwork been secured?
- If you provide any links to websites, make one last check that they are all live and go to the material you intend them to.
- Check the conference guidelines one more time. Check the style manual that you have been using to ensure conformity.
- Keep all your materials. Retain all your research notes, literature search results, correspondence, and emails about the project and more. In the days of very inexpensive electronic storage, there is no

reason to delete anything. You never know when you might need to refer to some work you have done.

- Consider going back to any reviewers that saw your material to see if they would like to take one more look at the "finished product."
- Most conferences do not ask presenters to include their poster number on the actual poster. Many times, it is on the board where you will hang the poster. If you know your number, a backup plan is to have it printed on a small piece of paper (in the same font size as the authors' names) that could be applied on site if need be. Scout a place on or around the poster where you could apply it.

As you move through the final stages of the process, if there are any last-minute changes or updates, remember to run through this list again.

Chapter 24

Submitting and Printing Your Poster

To finish the moment, to find the journey's end in every step of the road, to live the greatest number of good hours, is wisdom.
—*Ralph Waldo Emerson*

Your poster is complete. Now what? There are several routes to proceed. Check if the organizer wants to review your work for approval. Some conferences will now not only accept/reject posters, they may even edit and provide feedback and ask you to revise and resubmit.

The next step will be determined by whether the presentation will be paper/in person, an ePoster, or both.

If the presentation is digital, it is essential to confirm the all-important file specifications. Make sure the file format strictly conforms to the organizer's requirements. Confirm if the organizer requires your file format to be in RGB versus CMYK (which is connected to color replication). Also, confirm the dpi (or dots per inch) minimums and maximums.

If your poster will be digital, the organizer may provide a high-tech submission system. Or they may go low-tech and ask you to email it, likely via a zip file due to its file size. An organizer's submission systems may require you to register and log in important data about the authors, the content, and more. Many times, these systems may ask for keywords and other metadata. Pay very close attention to these requests for both accuracy of your name and affiliation but also to the all-important search terms for your work such as metadata. If your work is digital, they may want your material uploaded in component parts, such as your presentation separate from any video or animation files.

Always confirm receipt of your files with the organizer if there is not an auto-response from your upload. These large files can be caught in spam filters, so send a simple email afterward requesting confirmation of receipt.

If your poster will be presented in paper form, you will need to find a printer. If you have been working with your institution, they may do this in-house or be able to suggest a vendor, or they may have a print shop on campus. If not, a quick internet search of "academic poster printer" or the like will list several options. Shop around to see their pricing, turnaround time, customer ratings, and experience; do not simply choose the first one.

The larger companies make this incredibly easy to upload a file and proceed. Rush options are usually available. They also offer an option to see a digital proof. Depending on who created the poster and your confidence level, this may or may not be necessary. Also, if you used special characters, math symbols, or non-English language text, make sure you check these characters in the poster proof.

There are several options for paper including glossy, matte, vinyl, fabric, or more. Many people like the glitz of glossy stock and it is a good choice in some cases. But also consider the reflection that may occur under institutional lighting and that it is being read at a distance, possibly making your material less readable.

Also, these companies may offer to compose or lay out your poster for an additional charge.

Be mindful of the time to ship and the cost, if any. For a poster about 36" by 72" on matte paper, in the United States as of 2023 with no proof, the average cost of printing and shipping is between $80 and $125. These costs have many variables, so this is just a range for your information.

It is important to understand how you will be mounting your poster at the conference. Will it be tacked on a large metal stand with cork backing? If not, how will you adhere it to the surface?

Be prepared with an assortment of small metal thumbtacks and/or small bits of VELCRO (both sides) with sticky backing. Some people prefer Sticky Tack or another reusable putty-like, pressure-sensitive adhesive. Have too many options whatever you choose and always be prepared. The organizer may provide thumbtacks as well, but then again, they may not. Also be mindful of the weight of your poster. It can either sag in the center or curl at the edges. Perhaps practice putting it up at home to see what you will be dealing with.

Optional is a thin plexiglass sleeve that holds sheets of paper for a possible handout. These holders can be inviting to attendees to learn more when you are not present. Once again, organizers sometimes provide these holders.

Will you be flying/traveling to your presentation? How will the poster get there? There are some impressive portfolio tubes or carrying containers that will ensure no damage comes to your work. They are made of hard plastic with a neat carrying strap. Before you buy one, make sure no one in your department can lend you one. Make sure your poster will actually fit in such a carrier. Also, will it be allowed on a plane if you are flying there? Will there be a cost? Make sure you name is somewhere in the carrier in case it gets left behind.

When you are finalizing your file and getting it printed/submitted, do not wait until the last minute. Mistakes happen and living life on the edge can be exciting but may also mean the possibility of disaster. See your work printed ahead of time. Proof it. And carry it with you (as opposed to checking it as baggage or shipping it).

Finally, in case your file gets lost, or your poster destroyed, have a backup plan. Consider keeping an email in your draft folders with a zip file ready to resend if you need to. Ideally, entrust a person in your department with the zip file so that you can call at a moment's notice and have them resend it.

You have done all this work and made it to the promised land. Now it is showtime.

Part V

PRESENTING YOUR POSTER AND BEYOND

Chapter 25

Giving a Poster Presentation

A good orator is pointed and impassioned. —*Cicero*

Your findings and the message your poster presentation delivers are of paramount importance, but how you present yourself and interact with the attendees at an in-person event is very significant as well. Whether you are an experienced public speaker or dread talking to people about your work, here are some tips to present yourself and your ideas in the best light to maximize the impact your work has with the readers and in your field (Bond, 2023).

Be prepared:

- Know the times you need to hang or mount the poster. Know where to go. Conferences can be very large and specific areas are usually set aside for poster presentations and they can be off the beaten path, so scope out where you need to be ahead of time. Know when the poster has to come down and be prompt in its removal.
- Have all of your materials (tacks, VELCRO, Sticky Tack, handouts, holder, business cards, etc.) and be early. Know in advance what the conference organizer will provide, but always bring your own.
- Know the in-person hours for presentation and be early and be prepared. These times may be anywhere from half an hour to several hours. The best times for poster presentations at large conferences are during the middle of the schedule. The ones at the beginning are good, but people may miss them. At the end, people may be fatigued

of viewing posters. But to be honest, presenters rarely get to choose their times. Some conferences indicate that being present at some or all of the in-person times is optional but, if possible, attend every one without fail.

- Understand the judging process. Most poster presentations at conferences or meetings will include a review by a panel of judges or a jury of experts in the field. They will evaluate each poster on a host of factors. They may then present several awards, including best poster, most innovative work, best research, etc. These awards can be a great stepping stone in your career. The judges will use a scorecard or rubric to compare all of the posters. Normally they will rate a poster by various categories on a scale of one to five and determine a total for each presentation. Seek out the rubric that is used to understand what the judges are looking for. Typical categories for judging include originality, study design, study execution, validity of results, poster design and presentation, oral presentation, creativity, impact in the field, and overall results.

- Practice, practice, practice. If there will be a time when a group of judges or the like come around for your poster defense, have your comments prepared and, if possible, memorized. Think through common questions that might be asked as well as your possible answers. Ask a colleague to suggest some questions and practice the answers with them. You are looking to have your comments be informative but not wooden or sounding too rehearsed. This is your area and work you know well. Speak from the heart. The purpose to practice is for you to not miss salient points or ramble. *Practicing the answers to common questions is one of the keys to success.* When you are thinking through responses, also consider answers of different lengths. "Tell me about your work" might be answered in two sentences or a full three-minute explanation of what you accomplished. It would be up to you to assess the person asking the question and what their level of interest is.

- Dress for success. Conferences can be long days, seemingly a marathon. Many attendees understandably dress for comfort. However, remember the adage, "people judge a book by its cover." Assess what the unwritten dress code of the meeting is and shoot to be at the high end of it for your presentation. If it is a conference in a tropical climate, there is no need to wear formal attire, but dress up to your presentation, not down. Be neat, clean, and look your best. One last item—make sure you have comfortable shoes in case you have to stand. Many conferences provide a single chair. Be thankful there is one there but realize it may not be the most luxurious.

- Bring water or a drink in case you get dry mouth but be careful how much you consume. Know where the bathrooms are. Bring mints (not gum).

Know your audience:

- A diverse group of people will wander around poster presentations. Most conferences list on the badges that people wear who they are, where they are from, and sometimes their level in the organization. As you settle into the conference, understand the badge system and what the colors or titles mean. This will help you interact with attendees and their own level of experience. It is important to know if you are speaking with a board member of the organization or an exhibitor! Make sure your badge is correct with your degrees (if they list them) and affiliation. Some conferences have ribbons below the badge for various achievements. If one is "Poster Presenter," make sure you wear it with pride.
- Representatives from peer-review journals (such as the editors) or book publishers walk around poster presentations, sometimes looking for ideas or authors. Be prepared, if you meet one, with what your interest might be in turning your poster into an article, or maybe even a book. Get their contact information for future connection.
- Be aware of cultural, gender, and religious differences by region and country. Especially if you are outside the United States, understand expectations with hand shaking, business card presentation, and more. Err on the side of being professional rather than risk offense.
- For people who feel less comfortable with standing at a poster waiting for people to stop and talk to them, a temptation is to speak to the person at the poster next to them. Of course, introduce yourself to your neighbors. Learn about their work and talk about yours. Exchange contact information. But do not use them as a crutch to avoid talking to the people walking by. If you are constantly chatting with your neighbor, some people might think, "Oh they are busy, I

won't interrupt them." Be open and ready for people to engage you. That is why you are there.

- As people walk by, try not to stand in front of the most important parts (or any parts) of your work. Try to stand to the side so passersby can scan your title, subject, and visuals without having to look around you.

Making the connection:

- Many experienced conference attendees have developed a process for considering which posters they will read and which presenters to talk to. Schedules (and attention spans) usually restrict people from talking to and absorbing every poster. Many will quickly walk the presentation floor, glancing at the topics and maybe some graphics and then they will come back to the ones of interest to them. Some people will methodically work their way down an aisle and pick out presenters to talk to. Because of this, do not get discouraged if people walk by and do not stop or interact. Also, some attendees by their nature are not "people persons." They shy from the interaction as much as some presenters do. *Do not take it personally.* At the end of the day, you may not talk to a huge number of people, but when you do you are probably talking to highly connected, highly qualified, and highly interested attendees!
- Remember you are competing with a lot of things. There may be food or drinks being served. Talks or courses may be scheduled at the same time. You may be in a hallway and people are on a mission to get somewhere. Or they may just be tired from a long meeting. Be realistic—understand that you are not the only game in town.
- A big question is whether to engage (or try to, anyway) with people who are walking by to see if they will talk. Some people will feel uncomfortable with this, while others will think, "Why not?" It is a judgment call. People striding past do not want to be accosted like you are offering free samples at a mall. But by the same token, some attendees may be reticent to talk and just need a little nudge to stop and interact. It could be as little as you saying "good morning" or asking how their day is going. Another alternative is to make the time investment seem small on their end. "Want to hear very briefly about my work?" Others try, "Are you interested in XYZ as well?" When

you do this, be broad in your question and not as incredibly specific as the topic of your presentation. No matter your comfort level, try it a few times. See where you fall on the continuum. You will have some successes.

- As people stop, be deliberate in what happens next. If you feel comfortable, look the person in the eye and have a smile (or at least not a stern look) on your face. Eye contact can help make a powerful connection when done well. Make it easy for someone to get things started.
- Try to be upbeat and positive throughout your chat. Convey your sense of wonder about your project and more importantly about your chosen field of endeavor.
- Introduce yourself. This may seem commonsensical, but many times people forget. Decide if you will be John, John Bond, Dr. John Bond, John Bond from XYZ University, or something else. If you have several authors on your work, it may not be apparent who you are, especially if your badge gets flipped around.
- If you feel comfortable, try to use their name—either because they introduced themselves or because it is apparent on their badge. "Would you like me to walk you through my work, Dr. Smith?" This sets an inviting tone and builds a bridge to the attendee.
- Many conferences have an official language(s). English predominates in the United States but also in many other meetings. Be prepared to converse with someone who may have a language barrier to fully understanding your work. Sometimes relying on the written part of the poster may be a help.
- There are thousands of articles and hundreds of books on body language because it does matter. Most of us know the basics: have an open stance, with no crossed arms; do not stand too close; maintain good posture; mirror someone's actions. You do not need to make a study of body language but do be mindful of what it tells about you.
- Despite these guiding principles, be yourself. If you are not a jovial person or a talker, trying to be one just for the presentation may come off as forced or artificial. No matter your personality type, just try to be open and upbeat.
- The interaction will start in one of two ways—you can initiate or they will take the first step. You might begin with a greeting and an offer to explain your work. Wait for their next move. If they start things off, listen carefully to what they are saying or asking and do not just

launch into your nervously rehearsed summary. *Listening is the key to this interaction.*

- As you give various answers or descriptions, give your responses time to breathe. Leave pauses and give them time to absorb and ask more questions. A cardinal rule of interacting is not to interrupt the other person. No one enjoys a discussion with a person who has no periods or commas in their sentences. After you go through your points, ask them if you covered all the points they wanted you to? Suggest: "Would you like me to go into greater detail?"
- Answer the questions they ask, not what you have prepared. It may seem common sense, but sometimes people are intent on saying what they want to say, not responding to what they are asked. Some people may wish to take notes. If they do, give them time to do so and do not keep barraging them with information.
- If your work is by a group as opposed to just you, say "we" instead of "I" when describing your ideas.
- Know your content and work by heart. Do not read off the poster for any significant amount.
- Try to stand to the side and point at key graphics or data to help the attendee understand and locate what you are talking about.
- Be prepared for a wide range of questions, including those about your background, sources of funding, why you did the work, if you think it was a success, and what you would have done differently. Also, it is okay if you get asked a question you cannot answer. Offer to get back to them after you look into the matter.
- On average, plan to have your total interaction be under five minutes. It might be less or more and that is okay. But by keeping many of the interactions to a compact time frame, you will be able to talk to more people instead of being bogged down with one person for twenty or so minutes.
- Sometimes, there are exceptions. If a potential future employer or funder comes by and shows interest, expand your discussion time. Think through how to approach in conversation facts such as, "I'm defending my thesis in May" or "I'm in the second year of a postdoc."
- A challenge that presenters deal with is when they are engaged with one person, and another is hovering nearby or looks like they want to speak to you as well. This involves the art of reading the people and situation. Are you almost concluded with the one? Then perhaps nod

and acknowledge the other's presence. Have you just started with the current one? Then you may want to ask, "Do you want to join us? I just started to explain . . ." You then may need to catch them up on your introduction and what has been discussed. The unknown factor is how each person will react. You do not want to slight the person you are speaking with nor chase off the person in the wings.

- Be prepared and aware that things may not go smoothly. You may offer to walk someone through your work, and they cut you off and drift away. Or people may ignore you. Others might discuss or dismiss your work in several different ways. These will likely be the minority of interactions. Develop a thick skin to deal with these types of people and move on.
- It is a good practice for all people in this role to have a business card. Whether one is provided by your institution or you pay to create one (they are very inexpensive), they present a professional air and give people a simple way to follow up with you. When you give one, ask the person for theirs in return. If appropriate, make notes on the back of the card as to what you discussed and any intended follow-up. Also, be prepared to take notes in general, whether with a pad of paper and pen or digitally.

These are a lot of ideas and suggestions for making your poster presentation a success. Read through the list and then maybe revisit it the week or the day before your presentation. To help you better understand the many points above, here is a distillation.

The Top Ten Presentation Tips:

1. Be prepared.
2. Dress for success.
3. Know your audience.
4. Practice what you will say.
5. Smile and be positive.
6. Engage people who walk by.
7. Point at visuals or data in your poster.
8. Take five minutes or less per interaction.
9. Listen to what people say or ask.
10. Pause after you answer.

Of course, many of these points apply to in-person presentations. Yours may be digital or both. Some of the points apply to both. Some ePosters offer a question-and-answer period via audio or video as well. Apply the relevant ideas above to your presentation, no matter the format.

A side note: The 2020 pandemic changed many aspects of traditional in-person poster presentations. A couple of years' worth of conferences were canceled or moved online with varying degrees of success. As of late 2022, parts of the disruption seem to be behind us or at least better understood.

Nonetheless, it is probably wise to be prepared for possible future disruptions, whether from COVID-19 or something else. It seems to be the world we are living in.

First, accept that things may change from the announcement of the conference to the day you are standing on the floor speaking to attendees. If they do change, it is not because the organizers want this but because they are reacting to the news or local standards.

If you are traveling to the conference, consider getting trip or travel insurance. It does cost a bit more but can help you avoid a lot of hassle or expense if the situation changes.

Be prepared for in-person interaction with masks, wipes, or hand sanitizer.

Consider how much has changed with personal touch in the last ten years and even since the pandemic. At meetings, seeing people hug or touch a friend or colleague on the arm or shoulder was common. Handshakes were seemingly required for many people when they met. Now, so much of this seems of a bygone era. Some people feel well rid of these customs. Others might like to revive these in the "post" pandemic era. Whatever type of physical interaction person you are, be cognizant when you are the presenter and assume the person you are speaking with wants no handshake, fist bump, or similar type of connection. Be content with a smile and a greeting.

At the end of the day, the conference organizer (and the location where it is held) will drive the rules for these activities. You as the presenter should then be aware of the people you will be meeting and their varying levels of comfort.

In conclusion, this opportunity to present your poster has only positives for you and your career long-term. Suppose you stand in front of your poster for two hours and no one interacts with you? No worries. You have had your presentation accepted by the conference, created it, and presented it. Check that off your list. It was a success.

More likely, you will have been to an important conference, met exciting new people in your field, given a well-received presentation, and now you are ready to move on to bigger projects.

Chapter 26

Handouts, Networking, and Follow-Ups

There is nothing on this earth more to be prized than true friendship. —Thomas Aquinas

Posters are so much more than the actual presentation. They present many professional opportunities for you and your career.

To start with, a handout at your presentation is a valuable way to make a connection with attendees. This may take the form of a one-page (one- or two-sided) copied piece of paper that attendees can take with them. This handout should include the name of the conference and date of the poster, the poster title, all authors' names and affiliations, contact information for the authors, the abstract or summary, and any additional information you might want to provide such as the complete reference list or more data.

You might include a miniature version on your poster, or if it does not reproduce well because of being shrunk down, then just include a link to you and your work. It is a way for the attendee to connect afterward with you if they want to pursue something about what they saw. Consider making more copies than you think you need, maybe fifty or more. There are simple plastic sleeves or holders that can be attached to the poster. Add a helpful, "Take one" to the sleeve. Use bright paper for the copying. When you are at the poster, do not stand in front of your handout holder.

Other options for connecting with people are to add your email address, a website, or a QR code on the bottom corner of the poster. The

QR code or website might lead the user to your institutional home page or your personal website (see chapter 27 for more about this idea). List below the code where the link takes you. (If you are new to QR codes, there are websites that convert web addresses to a QR code.) You might also wish to display the entire poster at these websites. Check first with the organizer that this is permissible, or link to their site if they have made it publicly available. The links might also take them to your professional social networking site(s) such as ResearchGate or Academia .edu (more on this as well in chapter 27).

Giving the conference attendee a way to follow up with you about your work is important, but you will want a way to follow up with them as well. As mentioned in the previous chapter, it is a good practice for authors and researchers to have a business card. Whether one is provided by your institution or you pay to create one, it allows you to connect with someone in a simple way. When you give one, ask for theirs in return. You can leave several tacked outside the bottom of your poster for people to take if you are not there.

From your conference attendance, start to keep a list of people you meet. This list will be invaluable as you start to look for possible research partners, writing partners, or more. As discussed in chapter 18, having colleagues or others who can review your writing or work is crucial to improving and generating new and better ideas.

Follow up with these people in an email, clearly marking where you met and what your project was and their interest in it. You can also connect with them on sites like LinkedIn, Twitter, ResearchGate, and Academia.edu. Another suggestion is to keep a running list of these connections in a spreadsheet or the like. Track their name, affiliation, date, and where you met, their area of interest and specialty, and any other relevant information. However you track them, these contacts are important to stay in touch with and follow their careers and work.

To some, the concept of networking is an alien process associated with ambitious people. To others the skill comes naturally. But these connections, however easily made, are vital to career advancement and the growth of your ideas and work. Agree with it or not, the adage "It's not what you know; it's who you know" has been around for a long time for a reason.

Make sure you bring your poster back. Some institutions will adorn their hallways or common areas with past posters.

Also, a jury or committee may judge poster presentations. Honors and awards might be given for the conference. Connecting with these judges after the conference is another way to stay in touch with leaders in your field. Send them a note and thank them for their time (they are all volunteers) and tell them you enjoyed the experience.

Needless to say, if you are lucky enough to be honored in this way, congratulations. List it on your curriculum vitae and at your websites. This leads to our next chapter which discusses the importance of promoting your ideas and work.

Chapter 27

Promoting Your Work

If I am not for myself, who will be for me? —Rabbi Hillel

Please do not skip this chapter.

Many authors and researchers feel this is not (or should not be) part of what they do during the day.

With the many changes taking place in academic communication, the biggest threat to ideas and your work is obscurity. With the tsunami of content out there, authors (in addition to publishers, societies, and conference organizers) need to actively ensure that their work and research are available and being promoted in the marketplace of ideas.

You need to market and publicize your work, no questions asked. Some will push back on this idea in that it smacks of self-promotion. This may have been the attitude in the nineties or the aughts. But the world has changed, and you need to promote your work (and by extension, your career).

Here are some simple, inexpensive steps you can take to actively promote your work:

- Reach out to your contacts: Look through your contact list to find people you know who might be interested in your work. Send them an email, communication, or text that you will be presenting a poster at an upcoming conference. Ask them to stop by (give them the dates and times) if they will be there. If they will not, ask them to pass it along if anyone in their circle will be attending who might have an interest.

- Social media: Despite its recent fall from grace, social media still offers a great opportunity to connect with like-minded people. Think of it as a long-term effort. Choose only one channel, perhaps Twitter or LinkedIn, and concentrate on building your connections. Choose the one that clicks best with your discipline. Connections or followers are key. Plan on multiple postings at different times of the week and use appropriate hashtags, including photos of you at your poster (with a big smile). The conference will have an official hashtag to designate that meeting. Make sure you use it the whole time. Also, watch the conference's social media accounts and interact with their communications. Use quotations from your work or key facts or statistics to spark interest and dialogue, instead of simply posting about you. If anyone calls out your efforts on social media, respond to everyone with a comment or an acknowledgment.

- Academic social networking sites: Websites like ResearchGate and Academia.edu offer a great opportunity to promote your work and connect with others in their field. Members of the sites each have a user profile and can upload research output, including papers, data, presentations, and more. Google Scholar and other sites offer academics the chance to create a profile that is linked to their work. Claim your ORCID iD profile as well. Your institution likely has a profile for you at their site. With all of these, keep them up to date and link to your poster presentation and future efforts.

- Blogs: Having a blog or guest blogging can be a great opportunity to discuss your interests and research. A blog (when done right) is an investment in your future. Also, consider guest opportunities on podcasts and video channels in your field.

- Create short videos: Video usage has exploded in recent years. Very short (2- to 5-minute) videos can be created using any smartphone. These videos can be posted at YouTube, Vimeo, or TikTok and then shared on social media. Summarize your presentation or talk about why you got involved in your project. You can also make short videos at the conference of posters or presentations you experienced.

- Create a website: Every academic should have a site for themselves. With free or inexpensive website creation tools, it is easier and quicker than most people imagine. Shoot to have the site be your name. If that web address is already taken (as it was with me), then be creative. My alternative was www.booksbyjohnbond.com. Talk about your background, poster presentations, research interests, and link to or post all the work with which you are involved.

- LISTSERV or online forums: Once again, many subject areas have active forums for discussions. Participate in them for your long-term professional benefit. When possible, make mention of your presentation and link to it when appropriate.
- Use keywords: Ensure consistent use of keywords, not only with regard to your poster but when you are promoting your work, including all hashtags.

When you meet people at the presentation, check if they are on Twitter, LinkedIn, or the like. Consider listing your website or social media handle, etc. on the poster. List these items on your handout as well.

Time all these efforts with the conference and your presentation. On occasion, there is an embargo on some scholarly content, such as poster presentations. An embargo is a request by the conference organizer that the material not be released until a certain date or until certain conditions have been met. Check with the conference organizer.

All of these ideas have an eye toward your future research and writing career. They may seem like a lot for "just a poster," but they all will help build your footprint in your field and assist with your future endeavors.

Long term, your university or institution might help promote your work. Many have a public relations person specifically charged with issuing press releases or arranging media interviews about new research findings. Make sure to tag your institution in your posts/tweets, etc. And give them a heads-up that you will be at a conference and connecting your work with them on social media.

Do not skip this chapter or leave it for another day. Start now with efforts like signing up for social media or academic networking sites. Then start to make small incremental efforts every day.

Chapter 28

Growing Your Poster into an Article and Beyond

The desire to write grows with writing. —Desiderius Erasmus

Successfully giving a poster presentation is an important accomplishment, whether it is your first one or your tenth. But it is likely a stepping stone to greater academic communications. Peer-review journal articles may be next. Your poster is likely only part of a larger project or effort with which you are involved. The project may contain more significant work that you or your group can use as a basis for an article, or perhaps even more than one.

Peer-review journals have an endless need for new ideas and new manuscripts. Your experience with content creation, submission, acceptance, and promotion for your poster gives you a perfect launching point to consider this next step.

The skills acquired from creating and presenting posters have been foundational for many accomplished people in your field. If you review the longest curricula vitae of the most-lauded individuals, you will see poster presentations at the beginning of their careers, but also through their subsequent years.

If you proceed to writing and getting a journal article published, there are other places to go from there. Experienced writers, researchers, and academics have many other avenues open to them in scholarly communication. They can serve on the editorial boards of peer-review journals. Another step in a writing career might be to author or edit a monograph, textbook, or book. Authoring is also a step toward grant submission, which can be influential in one's future writing career. Grants can also have great impact on your career in general.

The society or organization that ran the conference where you presented is always in need of volunteer professionals on many committees. These organizations have extensive opportunities to help you grow in your profession and network with some of the best people in your field.

All of these ambitious ideas stem from the authoring of one poster presentation. Once again, this is the foundation for your future career and writing opportunities.

As you wind down from your effort and presentation, take a moment to think of what you would have done differently. Take stock of the things you did right and the things you would change.

Is it worth it? Poster creation and presentation takes time. Traveling to the conference costs time and money. All the while, your work back home may be piling up. Emails keep coming in.

If this effort is worth it, it is up to you. When you view your writing and academic career and the effect that any event may have on it over time, it may be difficult to appreciate because of the arc of time. All of your future accomplishments start with a single step, and a poster presentation is an important one most people in your situation have experienced.

You will develop a network of new and interesting people from outside your current sphere. You will be exposed to new ideas and perspectives that will help you grow. You will receive feedback on your writing, research, and presentation style that will be invaluable in the future. You will grow professionally.

This journey is well worth it. Bon voyage.

Sample Forms

Poster Presentation Planning Guide	
Task	**Target Date**
Define your topics/project.	
Write a succinct, focused abstract of about 250 words that summarizes your project.	
Formulate a tentative title for the poster.	
Detail the intended audience for your work.	
Research poster presentation opportunities, either in-person presentation or digital.	
* Connect with colleagues.	
* Search for call for poster presentation announcements.	
* Look at international, national, and regional conferences on related topics.	
* Decide on your best opportunity and submit your application.	
* Research funding opportunities at your institution, conference organizer, etc.	
Accepted!	
Closely review conference guidelines for poster creation.	
Develop a plan and timeline for the work ahead; adapt this document.	

Task	Target Date
Create a content outline using accepted subject headings like IMRaD.	
Write the first draft of the text paying close attention to suggested word counts.	
Designate which data and/or concepts you will express visually.	
Closely edit your work; rewrite if necessary.	
Consider showing a draft of your work to colleagues and ask for feedback.	
Decide who will lay out the poster: you, a freelancer, or someone at your institution.	
Will your choice be able to create high-quality graphics such as charts and figures?	
Review your first draft; suggest corrections. Review your final draft.	
Closely check conference guidelines to ensure that you are complying.	
Submit your poster to the organizer, if appropriate.	
Choose and submit your file to a poster printer.	
Upload your file to the conference submission system, if appropriate.	
Plan your brief explanation of your poster and common questions. Practice!	
Create a handout for your presentation.	
Bring appropriate supplies to hang your poster and to have onsite.	
Be prepared if pandemic restrictions are in place, bring masks, etc.	
Promote your work: social media, blogging, at websites, etc.	
Take photos and short videos on site, if permissible, and share.	
Network with attendees and other presenters. Get and give your business card.	
Consider if your poster and its related project can be turned into a journal article.	
Give more poster presentations!	
Customize your plan and add details and deadlines!	

Courtesy of John Bond, https://www.publishingfundamentals.com/

Final Checklist Prior to Leaving for the Conference	
Task	*Confirmed*
Confirm you have the acceptance notification from the organizer.	
Confirm your travel arrangements including hotel, air/transportation, etc.	
Ensure you are registered for the conference.	
Review the location, including the address, of the actual poster presentation.	
Verify the hours to set up your poster.	
Verify the hours of your presentation.	
Bring thumbtacks, VELCRO, Sticky Tack, handouts, holder, business cards.	
Run spell and grammar check on your text, tables, and figures.	
Check that the links to any websites or to a QR code are still live and valid.	
Review the conference organizer's conference guidelines.	
Poster printed out (if applicable)? Check for any printers' mistakes.	
Practice your short presentation as well as answers to common questions.	
Consider having a colleague review your finished print or digital poster.	
Check to ensure that your digital file was uploaded and the organizer acknowledged receipt.	
Have a backup digital copy of your poster on a zip drive or with a colleague.	
In case pandemic restrictions kick in, bring masks, hand sanitizer, etc.	
Have a plan for promoting your work.	
Take photos/videos while on site and post on social media, if permissible.	

Courtesy of John Bond, https://www.publishingfundamentals.com/

Further Reading

Andrade, C. "How to Write a Good Abstract for a Scientific Paper or Conference Presentation." *Indian Journal of Psychiatry* 53, no. 2 (April 2011): 172–75. https://doi.org/10.4103/0019-5545.82558

Block, Steven M. "Teaching Biophysics: Do's and Don'ts of Poster Presentation." *Biophysical Journal* 71, no. 6 (December 1996): 3527–29. https://doi.org/10.1016/S0006-3495(96)79549-8

Bond, John. *The Little Guide to Getting Your Journal Article Published: Simple Steps to Success.* Lanham, MD: Rowman & Littlefield, 2023.

"Effective Poster Presentations." Johns Hopkins University. https://ctei.jhu.edu/files/EffectivePosterPresentations-Handout.pdf (accessed September 27, 2022).

"ePosters." Technology Networks. http://www.eposters.net (accessed October 13, 2022).

"IMRAD." Wikipedia, The Free Encyclopedia. https://en.wikipedia.org/w/index.php?title=IMRAD&oldid=1075979834 (accessed September 27, 2022).

"iPosterSessions," aMuze! Interactive. https://ipostersessions.com/ (accessed October 13, 2022).

Bibliography

GENERAL RESOURCES

Beins, Bernard, and Agatha Beins. *Effective Writing in Psychology: Papers, Posters, and Presentations*. New York: Wiley-Blackwell, 2008.

Bond, John. "How to Give a Great Poster Presentation." YouTube video, 3:18. February 4, 2019. https://www.youtube.com/watch?v=grnSSMgE20o

Browner, Warren. *Publishing and Presenting Clinical Research*, 3rd ed. New York: Lippincott Williams & Wilkins, 2012.

Davis, Martha, Kaaron J. Davis, and Marion M. Dunnigan. *Scientific Papers and Presentations: Navigating Scientific Communication in Today's World*, 3rd ed. New York: Academic, 2012.

Erren, Thomas C., and Philip E. Bourne. "Ten Simple Rules for a Good Poster Presentation*." PLoS Computational Biology* 3, no. 5 (May 25, 2007): e102. https://doi.org/10.1371/journal.pcbi.0030102

Faulkes, Zen. *Better Posters: Plan, Design, and Present an Academic Poster*. London: Pelagic, 2021.

Gundogan, Buket, Kiron Koshy, Langhit Kurar, and Katharine Whitehurst. "How to Make an Academic Poster." *Annals of Medicine and Surgery* 11 (November 2016): 69–71. https://doi.org/10.1016/j.amsu.2016.09.001

Kiefer, Kate, Mike Palmquist, Luann Barnes, Marilyn Levine, and Don Zimmerman. "Poster Sessions." Writing@CSU. Colorado State University, 1999. https://writing.colostate.edu/guides/guide.cfm?guideid=78

Nicol, Adelheid A. M., and Penny M. Pexman. *Displaying Your Findings: A Practical Guide for Creating Figures, Posters, and Presentations*, 6th ed. Washington, DC: American Psychological Association, 2010.

Rowe, Nicholas. *Academic & Scientific Poster Presentation: A Modern Comprehensive Guide*, 1st ed. New York: Springer, 2017.

Sternberg, Robert, and Karin Sternberg. *The Psychologist's Companion for Undergraduates: A Guide to Success for College Students*, 1st ed. Cambridge: Cambridge University Press, 2017.

WRITING RESOURCES

Blum, Deborah. *A Field Guide for Science Writers: The Official Guide of the National Association of Science Writers*, 2nd ed. Oxford University Press, 2005.

Boice, Robert. *Professors as Writers: A Self-Help Guide to Productive Writing*. Stillwater, OK: New Forums, 1990.

Goodson, Patricia. *Becoming an Academic Writer: 50 Exercises for Paced, Productive, and Powerful Writing*, 2nd ed. Los Angeles: SAGE, 2012.

Heard, Stephen. *The Scientist's Guide to Writing: How to Write More Easily and Effectively throughout Your Career*. Princeton, NJ: Princeton University Press, 2016.

Hofmann, Angie. *Writing in the Biological Sciences: A Comprehensive Resource for Scientific Communication*, 3rd ed. New York: Oxford University Press, 2018.

Strunk, William, Jr. *The Elements of Style*, 4th ed. New York: Pearson, 2020.

Turabian, Kate L. *A Manual for Writers of Research Papers, Theses, and Dissertations*, 9th ed. Chicago: University of Chicago Press, 2018.

Resources

Bibliographic Management Software
Software Programs to Create Figures, Charts, and Tables
Style Manuals
Writing and Authoring Software

BIBLIOGRAPHIC MANAGEMENT SOFTWARE

EasyBib

http://www.easybib.com/

EndNote

https://endnote.com/

Mendeley

https://www.mendeley.com/

RefWorks

https://www.refworks.com/

Zotero

https://www.zotero.org

SOFTWARE PROGRAMS TO CREATE FIGURES, CHARTS, AND TABLES

Adobe Illustrator (graphic editor and design program)

https://www.adobe.com/products/illustrator.html

Canva (graphic design platform)

https://www.canva.com/

GraphPad by Dotmatics: Prism (analysis and graphing solution)

https://www.graphpad.com/features

MathWorks: MATLAB (plotting functions and data, implementation of algorithms)

https://www.mathworks.com/help/matlab/ref/figure.html

Mind the Graph (infographic creator)

https://mindthegraph.com/

Origin (data analysis and graphing software)

https://www.originlab.com/Origin

Presi (alternative to PowerPoint, versatile)

https://www.presi.com/

SigmaPlot (scientific graphing and data analysis)

https://systatsoftware.com/products/sigmaplot/

STYLE MANUALS (CHECK FOR THE CURRENT EDITION)

AMA Manual of Style: A Guide for Authors and Editors, 11th edition

http://www.amamanualofstyle.com/

The Chicago Manual of Style, 17th edition

https://www.chicagomanualofstyle.org

MLA Handbook, 9th edition

https://style.mla.org/

Publication Manual of the American Psychological Association, 7th edition

http://www.apastyle.org/

WRITING AND AUTHORING SOFTWARE

These are in addition to Apple Pages, Google Docs, and Microsoft Word

Evernote

https://evernote.com/

Grammarly

http://www.grammarly.com

OpenOffice

https://en.office.org/

Index

About the Author

John Bond has been connecting with writers and readers for over twenty-five years. He is a publishing consultant. John founded Riverwinds Consulting in 2015 to advise individuals, publishers, and trade societies or groups on topics dealing with book, journal, and digital publishing.

Previously, John worked for a publisher, starting as an editor, and eventually became the publisher and then chief content officer. He has overseen the publishing of over 500 books and 20,000 academic articles in peer-review journals in his career.

John is the host of the YouTube channel "Publishing Defined," which provides brief informative videos on publishing. The channel has over 6,000 subscribers, and the videos have been viewed over 445,000 times.

He is a proud member of the Textbook & Academic Authors Association. In his prior career, John was a librarian in K–12 education and continues to be a strong advocate for libraries as an evolving place for learning and education.

John is also the author of six books:

- *The Little Guide to Getting Your Journal Article Published: Simple Steps to Success*
- *The Little Guide to Getting Your Book Published: Simple Steps to Success*
- *Scholarly Publishing: A Primer*
- *The Request for Proposal in Publishing: Managing the RFP Process*

- *The Story of You: A Guide for Writing Your Personal Stories and Family History*
- *You Can Write and Publish a Book: Essential Information on How to Get Your Book Published, Second Edition*

Connect with John at Goodreads and see what is currently on his bedside table. He usually reads or listens to a book a week throughout the year.

John lives in New Jersey and owns more books than he will ever get to read but is trying.

Connect with John at his consultancy practice:
   https://www.riverwindsconsulting.com/
Find out about his work with individuals:
   https://www.publishingfundamentals.com/
See his other books at:
   https://www.booksbyjohnbond.com/
Connect with him on LinkedIn:
   https://www.linkedin.com/in/johnbondnj/
See any of his over one hundred videos on publishing on:
   https://www.youtube.com/JohnBond
Follow him on Twitter:
   @JohnHBond
Or email him at:
   jbond@RiverwindsConsulting.com